50 Korean Food Making Recipes for Home

By: Kelly Johnson

Table of Contents

- Kimchi (Traditional Fermented Napa Cabbage)
- Bulgogi (Marinated Beef BBQ)
- Bibimbap (Mixed Rice Bowl)
- Japchae (Stir-Fried Sweet Potato Noodles)
- Kimbap (Seaweed Rice Rolls)
- Tteokbokki (Spicy Rice Cakes)
- Samgyeopsal (Grilled Pork Belly)
- Galbi (Grilled Marinated Short Ribs)
- Sundubu-jjigae (Soft Tofu Stew)
- Kimchi Jjigae (Kimchi Stew)
- Dakgalbi (Spicy Stir-Fried Chicken)
- Haemul Pajeon (Seafood Pancake)
- Bulgogi Jeongol (Beef and Vegetable Hot Pot)
- Dolsot Bibimbap (Stone Pot Mixed Rice)
- Mandu (Dumplings)
- Hobakjuk (Pumpkin Porridge)
- Doenjang Jjigae (Soybean Paste Stew)
- Bossam (Boiled Pork Wraps)
- Gimbap (Korean Seaweed Rolls)
- Yukgaejang (Spicy Beef Soup)
- Ojingeo Bokkeum (Spicy Stir-Fried Squid)
- Banchan (Assorted Side Dishes)
- Kongnamul Muchim (Seasoned Soybean Sprouts)
- Jeyuk Bokkeum (Spicy Stir-Fried Pork)
- Gochujang Samgyeopsal (Grilled Pork Belly with Chili Paste)
- Eomuk Bokkeum (Stir-Fried Fish Cake)
- Gyeran Jjim (Steamed Egg)
- Kimchi Fried Rice
- Dakkochi (Grilled Chicken Skewers)
- Jajangmyeon (Noodles in Black Bean Sauce)
- Budae Jjigae (Army Stew)
- Sannakji (Live Octopus)
- Kalguksu (Handmade Noodle Soup)
- Ssambap (Lettuce Wraps with Rice)
- Hotteok (Sweet Stuffed Pancakes)
- Gamjatang (Spicy Pork Bone Soup)

- Ojingeochae Bokkeum (Stir-Fried Dried Squid)
- Nakji Bokkeum (Stir-Fried Baby Octopus)
- Kimchi Mandu (Kimchi Dumplings)
- Mul Naengmyeon (Cold Buckwheat Noodles in Broth)
- Yangnyeom Tongdak (Korean Fried Chicken)
- Ganjang Gejang (Soy Sauce Marinated Crabs)
- Gopchang Jeongol (Beef Intestine Hot Pot)
- Guljeon (Oyster Pancakes)
- Dubu Kimchi (Stir-Fried Tofu with Kimchi)
- Dak Bulgogi (Spicy Chicken BBQ)
- Saengseon Jeon (Pan-Fried Fish Cakes)
- Yukhoe (Korean Beef Tartare)
- Gaji Namul (Seasoned Eggplant)
- Maeuntang (Spicy Fish Stew)

Kimchi (Traditional Fermented Napa Cabbage)

Ingredients:

- 1 napa cabbage (about 2 pounds)
- 1/2 cup sea salt
- 1 tablespoon sugar
- 1 cup water
- 1 tablespoon grated ginger
- 4 cloves garlic, minced
- 2 tablespoons fish sauce or Korean salted shrimp paste (saeujeot)
- 2 tablespoons Korean red pepper flakes (gochugaru)
- 4 green onions, chopped
- 1 small carrot, julienned (optional)

Instructions:

1. **Prepare the cabbage:**
   - Cut the napa cabbage lengthwise into quarters and remove the core. Cut each quarter crosswise into 2-inch pieces.
   - Place the cabbage pieces in a large bowl and sprinkle with sea salt. Massage the salt into the cabbage leaves to help soften them. Add enough water to cover the cabbage. Place a plate on top to keep the cabbage submerged. Let it sit for 1-2 hours, tossing occasionally.
2. **Rinse and drain:**
   - After 1-2 hours, rinse the cabbage thoroughly under cold water to remove excess salt. Drain well and set aside.
3. **Make the kimchi paste:**
   - In a small bowl, combine sugar and 1 cup of water. Stir until the sugar is dissolved.
   - Add grated ginger, minced garlic, fish sauce or salted shrimp paste, Korean red pepper flakes (gochugaru), green onions, and julienned carrot (if using). Mix well to make a paste-like consistency.
4. **Mix the cabbage and paste:**
   - Gently squeeze the excess water from the cabbage and transfer it to a large mixing bowl.
   - Add the kimchi paste to the cabbage. Wear gloves if desired and mix thoroughly, ensuring the paste coats each piece of cabbage evenly.
5. **Ferment the kimchi:**
   - Pack the kimchi into a clean glass jar or airtight container, pressing down firmly to remove any air bubbles. Leave some space at the top as kimchi will expand during fermentation.
   - Seal the jar tightly and let it sit at room temperature for 1-2 days to begin the fermentation process. During this time, open the lid to release gases produced by fermentation and press down on the kimchi with a clean spoon.

6. **Store and age:**
   - After 1-2 days, transfer the jar to the refrigerator. Let the kimchi continue to ferment for at least 3-5 days before tasting. The flavor will develop further as it ages.
7. **Serve:**
   - Enjoy your homemade kimchi as a side dish, in rice dishes, soups, or stir-fries. It can be stored in the refrigerator for several weeks to months, developing deeper flavors over time.

Kimchi is versatile and can be adjusted according to personal taste preferences. Experiment with different vegetables or spice levels to create your unique variation of this iconic Korean dish.

Bulgogi (Marinated Beef BBQ)

Ingredients:

- 1 pound thinly sliced beef (rib eye or sirloin)
- 1/2 onion, thinly sliced
- 2 green onions, chopped
- 3 cloves garlic, minced
- 1/4 cup soy sauce
- 2 tablespoons brown sugar
- 1 tablespoon sesame oil
- 1 tablespoon rice wine or mirin
- 1 tablespoon sesame seeds
- 1/4 teaspoon black pepper
- 1 tablespoon vegetable oil (for cooking)
- Optional: 1 pear, grated (for tenderizing the meat)

Instructions:

1. **Prepare the marinade:**
    - In a bowl, combine soy sauce, brown sugar, sesame oil, rice wine or mirin, minced garlic, sesame seeds, and black pepper. Mix well until the sugar is dissolved. If using pear, grate it and add it to the marinade for extra tenderness.
2. **Marinate the beef:**
    - Place the thinly sliced beef in a large bowl or resealable plastic bag.
    - Pour the marinade over the beef, making sure all pieces are coated evenly. Add sliced onions and chopped green onions to the marinade as well.
    - Cover the bowl or seal the bag and refrigerate for at least 1 hour, or ideally overnight for the flavors to develop.
3. **Cook the Bulgogi:**
    - Heat a large skillet or grill pan over medium-high heat. Add vegetable oil to coat the surface.
    - Remove the marinated beef from the refrigerator and let it come to room temperature.
    - Working in batches if necessary, cook the beef slices in a single layer until browned and cooked through, about 2-3 minutes per side.
    - Reserve any remaining marinade for basting or serve it as a sauce on the side.
4. **Serve:**
    - Transfer the cooked Bulgogi to a serving platter or individual plates.
    - Garnish with additional sesame seeds and chopped green onions if desired.
    - Serve Bulgogi with steamed rice and Korean side dishes (banchan) such as Kimchi, pickled vegetables, or lettuce leaves for wrapping (ssam).

Bulgogi is delicious served hot off the grill or pan-fried, with its tender and flavorful meat complemented by the sweet-savory marinade. Enjoy this iconic Korean BBQ dish with friends and family!

Bibimbap (Mixed Rice Bowl)

Ingredients:

For the Bibimbap Sauce (Gochujang Sauce):

- 3 tablespoons gochujang (Korean red pepper paste)
- 1 tablespoon sesame oil
- 1 tablespoon soy sauce
- 1 tablespoon honey or sugar
- 1 tablespoon rice vinegar
- 1 clove garlic, minced
- 1 tablespoon water

For the Bibimbap:

- 2 cups cooked short-grain rice (preferably Korean or sushi rice)
- 1 cup bean sprouts, blanched
- 1 cup spinach, blanched and seasoned with sesame oil and salt
- 1 cup carrots, julienned and stir-fried
- 1 cup zucchini, julienned and stir-fried
- 1 cup shiitake mushrooms, thinly sliced and stir-fried
- 1/2 pound beef (rib eye or sirloin), thinly sliced and marinated (optional)
- 4 eggs
- Sesame seeds, for garnish
- Vegetable oil, for cooking

Instructions:

1. **Prepare the Bibimbap Sauce (Gochujang Sauce):**
   - In a small bowl, combine gochujang, sesame oil, soy sauce, honey or sugar, rice vinegar, minced garlic, and water. Mix well until smooth. Adjust the sweetness or spiciness according to your preference. Set aside.
2. **Cook the rice:**
   - Cook the short-grain rice according to package instructions. Ideally, use a Korean or sushi rice variety for a sticky texture suitable for Bibimbap.
3. **Prepare the vegetables:**
   - Blanch bean sprouts in boiling water for 1-2 minutes. Drain and season lightly with salt and sesame oil.
   - Blanch spinach in boiling water for 30 seconds to 1 minute until wilted. Drain, squeeze out excess water, and season with sesame oil and salt.
   - Julienne carrots and zucchini. Stir-fry each vegetable separately in a little vegetable oil until tender-crisp. Season lightly with salt.
4. **Cook the beef (optional):**

- Marinate thinly sliced beef (rib eye or sirloin) in a mixture of soy sauce, sesame oil, minced garlic, and a pinch of sugar for at least 15 minutes. Stir-fry in a hot pan until cooked through. Set aside.

5. **Fry the eggs:**
   - Heat a small amount of vegetable oil in a non-stick skillet over medium heat. Fry eggs sunny-side-up or over-easy, keeping the yolks runny.
6. **Assemble Bibimbap:**
   - Divide the cooked rice among serving bowls.
   - Arrange the blanched and stir-fried vegetables, cooked beef (if using), and fried eggs on top of the rice in sections or circles.
7. **Serve:**
   - Drizzle Bibimbap Sauce (Gochujang Sauce) over the ingredients according to your taste.
   - Garnish with sesame seeds.
   - To eat, mix everything together thoroughly before enjoying, ensuring the egg yolk mixes with the rice and vegetables for a delicious blend of flavors and textures.

Bibimbap is customizable based on personal preferences and the availability of ingredients. It's a hearty and satisfying dish that offers a wonderful balance of flavors and textures, making it a favorite in Korean cuisine.

Japchae (Stir-Fried Sweet Potato Noodles)

Ingredients:

- 200g (7 oz) sweet potato noodles (dangmyeon)
- 1 small onion, thinly sliced
- 1 carrot, julienned
- 1 red bell pepper, thinly sliced
- 1/2 cup spinach
- 4-5 shiitake mushrooms, thinly sliced
- 2-3 green onions, cut into 2-inch pieces
- 2 cloves garlic, minced
- 2 tablespoons soy sauce
- 1 tablespoon sesame oil
- 1 tablespoon sugar
- 1 tablespoon vegetable oil
- Sesame seeds, for garnish
- Salt and pepper, to taste

Instructions:

1. **Prepare sweet potato noodles:**
    - Bring a large pot of water to a boil. Add sweet potato noodles and cook for 6-7 minutes, or until noodles are soft and translucent.
    - Drain and rinse noodles under cold water to stop cooking. Cut noodles with kitchen scissors into shorter lengths for easier handling. Set aside.
2. **Prepare vegetables:**
    - Blanch spinach in boiling water for 30 seconds, then rinse under cold water and squeeze out excess water. Cut into bite-sized pieces.
    - Heat vegetable oil in a large pan or wok over medium-high heat. Add minced garlic and stir-fry until fragrant, about 30 seconds.
    - Add sliced onion, carrot, red bell pepper, and shiitake mushrooms. Stir-fry for 3-4 minutes until vegetables are tender-crisp.
3. **Combine noodles and vegetables:**
    - Add cooked sweet potato noodles to the pan with vegetables. Stir in soy sauce, sesame oil, and sugar. Mix well to evenly coat noodles and vegetables.
    - Taste and adjust seasoning with salt and pepper if needed. Stir-fry for another 2-3 minutes until heated through.
4. **Finish and serve:**
    - Remove from heat and transfer Japchae to a serving platter.
    - Garnish with sesame seeds and sliced green onions.
    - Serve warm or at room temperature as a side dish or main course. Japchae can be enjoyed on its own or alongside other Korean dishes.

Japchae is known for its chewy texture from the sweet potato noodles and its savory-sweet flavor from the soy sauce and sesame oil seasoning. It's a versatile dish that can be customized with additional vegetables or protein such as beef, chicken, or tofu. Enjoy making and sharing this delicious Korean classic!

Kimbap (Seaweed Rice Rolls)

Ingredients:

- 4 sheets of dried seaweed (gim/nori)
- 4 cups cooked short-grain rice (Korean or sushi rice)
- 1 tablespoon sesame oil
- 1 tablespoon sesame seeds
- 1/2 teaspoon salt
- 4 strips of pickled yellow radish (danmuji), thinly sliced lengthwise
- 4 strips of cooked fish cake (eomuk), thinly sliced lengthwise
- 4 strips of cucumber, julienned
- 4 strips of carrot, julienned and stir-fried
- 4 strips of spinach, blanched and seasoned with sesame oil and salt
- 4 strips of cooked beef or ham (optional)
- 4 eggs, beaten and cooked into thin omelets
- Mayonnaise or seasoned mustard (optional)

Instructions:

1. **Prepare the ingredients:**
   - Cook short-grain rice according to package instructions. While still warm, season with sesame oil, sesame seeds, and salt. Mix well and let it cool to room temperature.
2. **Prepare the fillings:**
   - Julienne cucumber, carrot, and any other vegetables. Stir-fry carrots briefly with a little oil and salt until tender-crisp. Blanch spinach and season lightly with sesame oil and salt. Cook eggs into thin omelets, cut into strips.
3. **Assemble Kimbap:**
   - Place a bamboo sushi mat on a clean surface. Lay a sheet of dried seaweed (gim/nori) shiny side down on the mat.
   - Spread a thin layer of seasoned rice evenly over the seaweed, leaving a 1-inch border at the top.
   - Arrange strips of pickled yellow radish, fish cake, cucumber, carrot, spinach, and any optional ingredients horizontally across the center of the rice.
4. **Roll Kimbap:**
   - Lift the bottom edge of the bamboo mat with both hands, rolling it over the filling, using your fingers to hold the filling in place.
   - Continue rolling tightly until you reach the top edge. Dampen the top edge of the seaweed with a little water to seal the roll.
   - With a sharp knife, slice the rolled Kimbap into bite-sized pieces, about 1 inch thick.
5. **Serve:**
   - Arrange sliced Kimbap on a serving platter. Serve with mayonnaise or seasoned mustard on the side for dipping if desired.

Kimbap is a versatile dish where you can adjust the fillings according to your preference or what you have on hand. It's perfect for a light meal, picnic, or party, and it showcases the vibrant colors and flavors of Korean cuisine. Enjoy making and sharing this delicious Korean seaweed rice roll!

Tteokbokki (Spicy Rice Cakes)

Ingredients:

- 1 pound (450g) cylinder-shaped rice cakes (tteok)
- 4 cups water
- 5-6 large dried anchovies, heads and guts removed (optional, for broth)
- 1 piece dried kelp (about 6x6 inches), optional (for broth)
- 1/2 onion, thinly sliced
- 1/2 cup cabbage, thinly sliced
- 2-3 green onions, cut into 2-inch pieces
- 1/2 cup Korean fish cakes, sliced into strips (optional)
- 2 tablespoons vegetable oil
- Sesame seeds, for garnish

For the Tteokbokki Sauce:

- 3 tablespoons gochujang (Korean red pepper paste)
- 1 tablespoon gochugaru (Korean red pepper flakes), adjust to taste
- 2 tablespoons soy sauce
- 1 tablespoon sugar
- 1 tablespoon honey or corn syrup
- 2 cloves garlic, minced
- 1 teaspoon sesame oil
- 1 cup water (reserved from anchovy-kelp broth, or plain water)

Instructions:

1. **Prepare the anchovy-kelp broth (optional):**
   - In a pot, bring 4 cups of water to a boil. Add dried anchovies and dried kelp (if using). Boil for 5 minutes, then remove the anchovies and kelp. Reserve 1 cup of the broth for the sauce.
2. **Soak the rice cakes:**
   - If using dried rice cakes, soak them in warm water for 20-30 minutes until they soften slightly. Drain before cooking.
   - If using frozen rice cakes, thaw them in cold water until they separate.
3. **Make the Tteokbokki sauce:**
   - In a bowl, combine gochujang, gochugaru, soy sauce, sugar, honey or corn syrup, minced garlic, sesame oil, and 1 cup of water (either from the anchovy-kelp broth or plain water). Mix well until smooth.
4. **Cook the Tteokbokki:**
   - Heat vegetable oil in a large pan or wok over medium-high heat. Add sliced onion and cabbage, stir-fry for 2-3 minutes until slightly softened.
   - Add the rice cakes and Korean fish cakes (if using). Stir-fry for another 2-3 minutes.

- Pour the Tteokbokki sauce over the ingredients in the pan. Stir well to coat everything evenly.
5. **Simmer and thicken:**
    - Bring the mixture to a boil, then reduce heat to medium-low. Simmer uncovered for 10-15 minutes, stirring occasionally, until the sauce thickens and rice cakes are chewy and cooked through.
    - Add green onions during the last few minutes of cooking.
6. **Serve:**
    - Transfer Tteokbokki to a serving dish. Sprinkle with sesame seeds for garnish.
    - Serve hot as a snack or side dish. Enjoy the spicy-sweet flavors of homemade Tteokbokki!

Tteokbokki is best enjoyed fresh and hot, with its addictive combination of chewy rice cakes and flavorful sauce. Adjust the spiciness to your liking by adding more or less gochugaru. It's a comforting dish that's perfect for sharing with family and friends.

Samgyeopsal (Grilled Pork Belly)

Ingredients:

- 1 pound (450g) pork belly, thinly sliced
- Fresh lettuce leaves, for wrapping
- Ssamjang (Korean dipping sauce)
- Kimchi and other banchan (Korean side dishes)

For the marinade (optional):

- 3 tablespoons soy sauce
- 2 tablespoons sugar
- 1 tablespoon rice wine or mirin
- 1 tablespoon sesame oil
- 2 cloves garlic, minced
- 1 teaspoon black pepper

Instructions:

1. **Prepare the pork belly:**
   - If you're using a marinade, combine soy sauce, sugar, rice wine or mirin, sesame oil, minced garlic, and black pepper in a bowl. Mix well until sugar dissolves. Marinate the pork belly slices in this mixture for at least 30 minutes, or overnight in the refrigerator for deeper flavor.
2. **Preheat the grill:**
   - Heat a grill or grill pan over medium-high heat until hot. You can also use a tabletop Korean BBQ grill for an authentic experience.
3. **Grill the pork belly:**
   - Place the marinated pork belly slices on the hot grill. Cook for 2-3 minutes on each side, or until the pork belly is cooked through and nicely charred. Pork belly cooks quickly due to its thin slices, so keep an eye on it to avoid overcooking.
4. **Serve:**
   - Transfer the grilled pork belly to a serving plate.
   - Serve immediately with fresh lettuce leaves for wrapping.
   - Accompany with ssamjang (Korean dipping sauce) and various banchan (Korean side dishes) such as kimchi, pickled radish, and seasoned vegetables.
5. **Enjoy:**
   - To eat, take a lettuce leaf, add a piece of grilled pork belly, a small spoonful of ssamjang, and any desired banchan. Wrap it up and enjoy the burst of flavors and textures.

Samgyeopsal is often enjoyed as a communal meal where everyone at the table participates in grilling their own meat and assembling their wraps. It's a delicious and interactive dining experience that's popular among Koreans and Korean BBQ enthusiasts worldwide.

Galbi (Grilled Marinated Short Ribs)

Ingredients:

- 2 pounds (about 1 kg) beef short ribs, flanken-cut (cut across the bone into thin slices)
- 1/2 cup soy sauce
- 1/4 cup brown sugar
- 3 tablespoons mirin or rice wine
- 2 tablespoons sesame oil
- 4 cloves garlic, minced
- 1 small onion, grated
- 1 tablespoon ginger, grated
- 1/4 teaspoon black pepper
- Optional: 1 Asian pear, grated (for tenderizing)

Instructions:

1. **Prepare the marinade:**
    - In a bowl, combine soy sauce, brown sugar, mirin or rice wine, sesame oil, minced garlic, grated onion, grated ginger, and black pepper. If using, grate an Asian pear and add it to the marinade for additional flavor and tenderizing properties.
2. **Marinate the short ribs:**
    - Place the beef short ribs in a large resealable plastic bag or a shallow dish.
    - Pour the marinade over the ribs, making sure they are well-coated. Massage the marinade into the meat.
    - Seal the bag or cover the dish with plastic wrap. Marinate in the refrigerator for at least 4 hours, preferably overnight for the flavors to develop.
3. **Grill the Galbi:**
    - Preheat your grill to medium-high heat.
    - Remove the marinated short ribs from the refrigerator and let them come to room temperature.
    - Grill the ribs for 3-4 minutes per side, or until they are caramelized and cooked to your desired doneness. You can also cook them on a stovetop grill pan or broil them in the oven.
4. **Serve:**
    - Transfer the grilled Galbi to a serving platter.
    - Optionally, garnish with sesame seeds and sliced green onions for added flavor and presentation.
    - Serve hot with steamed rice, lettuce leaves for wrapping, ssamjang (Korean dipping sauce), and various banchan (Korean side dishes) such as kimchi and pickled vegetables.
5. **Enjoy:**

- To eat, wrap a piece of Galbi in a lettuce leaf, add a spoonful of ssamjang, and any desired banchan. Alternatively, enjoy the Galbi with steamed rice and a side of kimchi for a complete meal.

Galbi is a delightful dish that combines tender meat with a rich marinade, showcasing the sweet-savory flavors characteristic of Korean cuisine. It's perfect for gatherings and celebrations, offering a memorable dining experience with friends and family.

Sundubu-jjigae (Soft Tofu Stew)

Ingredients:

- 1 block (about 14 oz) soft tofu (sundubu), cut into cubes
- 1/2 onion, thinly sliced
- 1/2 zucchini, thinly sliced
- 4-5 shiitake mushrooms, thinly sliced
- 1/2 cup kimchi, chopped (optional, for kimchi sundubu-jjigae)
- 100g (3.5 oz) pork belly or beef, thinly sliced (optional)
- 2-3 cloves garlic, minced
- 2 green onions, chopped (separate white and green parts)
- 1 tablespoon gochugaru (Korean red pepper flakes), adjust to taste
- 1 tablespoon gochujang (Korean red pepper paste)
- 1 tablespoon soy sauce
- 1 teaspoon sesame oil
- 1 teaspoon vegetable oil
- 2 cups anchovy or vegetable broth
- 1 egg (optional), for topping
- Salt and pepper, to taste
- Sesame seeds, for garnish

Instructions:

1. **Prepare the ingredients:**
     - Cut the soft tofu into cubes and set aside.
     - Thinly slice the onion, zucchini, and shiitake mushrooms.
     - If using meat, thinly slice pork belly or beef. Chop kimchi if making kimchi sundubu-jjigae.
2. **Make the broth:**
     - Heat vegetable oil in a pot over medium heat. Add minced garlic and white parts of green onions. Stir-fry for 1-2 minutes until fragrant.
     - Add gochugaru (Korean red pepper flakes) and gochujang (Korean red pepper paste). Stir well to combine with the garlic and onions.
3. **Cook the stew:**
     - Add sliced onion and zucchini to the pot. Stir-fry for a few minutes until vegetables start to soften.
     - If using meat, add it to the pot and cook until lightly browned.
     - Pour in anchovy or vegetable broth. Bring to a boil, then reduce heat to medium-low.
4. **Add tofu and season:**
     - Carefully add the cubed soft tofu to the stew. Gently stir to combine with the other ingredients.
     - Season with soy sauce and sesame oil. Taste the broth and adjust seasoning with salt and pepper if needed.

5. **Simmer and finish:**
   - Let the stew simmer for about 5-7 minutes, allowing the flavors to meld together and the tofu to heat through.
   - If using kimchi, add it to the stew and simmer for an additional 2-3 minutes.
   - Optionally, crack an egg into the stew and let it cook until the white is set but the yolk is still runny.
6. **Serve:**
   - Garnish Sundubu-jjigae with chopped green onions and sesame seeds.
   - Serve hot, directly from the pot, with steamed rice on the side.

Sundubu-jjigae is best enjoyed piping hot, with its silky soft tofu and spicy broth providing warmth and comfort. It's a popular Korean dish that's perfect for cold days or whenever you crave a flavorful and satisfying stew.

Kimchi Jjigae (Kimchi Stew)

Ingredients:

- 2 cups well-fermented kimchi, chopped
- 200g (7 oz) pork belly or pork shoulder, thinly sliced (optional)
- 1/2 onion, thinly sliced
- 1/2 block (about 7 oz) firm tofu, cut into cubes
- 2-3 garlic cloves, minced
- 1 tablespoon gochugaru (Korean red pepper flakes), adjust to taste
- 1 tablespoon gochujang (Korean red pepper paste)
- 1 tablespoon soy sauce
- 1 teaspoon sesame oil
- 1 teaspoon vegetable oil
- 3 cups anchovy or vegetable broth, or water
- 1 green onion, chopped (optional, for garnish)
- Sesame seeds, for garnish (optional)

Instructions:

1. **Prepare the ingredients:**
   - Chop the kimchi into bite-sized pieces if it's not already chopped.
   - Thinly slice the onion and mince the garlic.
   - Cut tofu into cubes and set aside.
2. **Cook the stew:**
   - Heat vegetable oil in a large pot over medium heat. Add minced garlic and stir-fry for about 1 minute until fragrant.
   - Add sliced pork (if using) to the pot and cook until lightly browned.
3. **Add kimchi and seasonings:**
   - Add chopped kimchi to the pot. Stir-fry with the pork (if using) for about 3-4 minutes until it starts to soften and become fragrant.
   - Add gochugaru (Korean red pepper flakes) and gochujang (Korean red pepper paste). Mix well to coat the kimchi evenly.
4. **Simmer the stew:**
   - Pour in anchovy or vegetable broth (or water) into the pot. Bring the mixture to a boil, then reduce heat to medium-low.
5. **Add tofu and finish cooking:**
   - Add sliced onion and cubed tofu to the pot. Stir gently to combine with the kimchi mixture.
   - Let the stew simmer for about 15-20 minutes, stirring occasionally, until the flavors meld together and the tofu is heated through.
6. **Adjust seasoning and serve:**
   - Taste the stew and adjust seasoning with soy sauce if needed. If you prefer a spicier stew, you can add more gochugaru.
   - Garnish with chopped green onion and sesame seeds if desired.

7. **Serve hot:**
   - Serve Kimchi Jjigae hot, directly from the pot. It's typically enjoyed with a bowl of steamed rice and perhaps some additional banchan (Korean side dishes) like kimchi or pickled vegetables.

Kimchi Jjigae is a comforting dish that showcases the bold flavors of kimchi and is perfect for warming up on cold days. It's a versatile dish that can be adjusted to suit your taste preferences by varying the amount of spice or adding different ingredients. Enjoy this delicious taste of Korean cuisine!

Dakgalbi (Spicy Stir-Fried Chicken)

Ingredients:

- 500g (1.1 lbs) boneless, skinless chicken thighs or breasts, cut into bite-sized pieces
- 2 cups cabbage, chopped
- 1 sweet potato, peeled and thinly sliced
- 1 small carrot, peeled and thinly sliced
- 1/2 onion, thinly sliced
- 2-3 green onions, cut into 2-inch pieces
- 4-5 perilla leaves (optional), cut into strips
- 2 tablespoons vegetable oil

For the marinade/sauce:

- 3 tablespoons gochujang (Korean red pepper paste)
- 1 tablespoon gochugaru (Korean red pepper flakes), adjust to taste
- 2 tablespoons soy sauce
- 1 tablespoon mirin or rice wine
- 1 tablespoon sugar
- 2 cloves garlic, minced
- 1 teaspoon sesame oil

Instructions:

1. **Marinate the chicken:**
   - In a bowl, combine gochujang, gochugaru, soy sauce, mirin or rice wine, sugar, minced garlic, and sesame oil to make the marinade/sauce.
   - Add the chicken pieces to the marinade and mix well. Let it marinate for at least 30 minutes, or refrigerate for up to 2 hours for more flavor.
2. **Prepare the vegetables:**
   - Chop cabbage, sweet potato, carrot, onion, green onions, and perilla leaves (if using) into bite-sized pieces.
3. **Cook Dakgalbi:**
   - Heat vegetable oil in a large pan or skillet over medium-high heat.
   - Add marinated chicken pieces to the pan, spreading them out into an even layer. Cook for about 5-6 minutes, stirring occasionally, until chicken is almost cooked through.
4. **Add vegetables and sauce:**
   - Add chopped cabbage, sweet potato, carrot, onion, and green onions to the pan with the chicken. Stir-fry for another 5-7 minutes, or until vegetables are tender and chicken is fully cooked.
5. **Finish and serve:**
   - Add perilla leaves (if using) to the pan and stir to combine with the chicken and vegetables.

- Taste and adjust seasoning if needed. You can add more gochugaru for extra spiciness or a touch of sugar to balance the flavors.
- Serve hot directly from the pan, garnished with additional chopped green onions or sesame seeds if desired.

6. **Serve with:**
   - Dakgalbi is traditionally served with steamed rice and enjoyed with additional banchan (Korean side dishes) such as kimchi and pickled vegetables.

Dakgalbi is a flavorful and satisfying dish that combines tender chicken, crunchy vegetables, and a spicy-sweet sauce. It's perfect for sharing with family and friends, especially during gatherings or special occasions. Enjoy the delicious taste of Korean cuisine with this Dakgalbi recipe!

Haemul Pajeon (Seafood Pancake)

Ingredients:

- 1 cup all-purpose flour
- 1 cup water
- 1 egg
- 1/2 teaspoon salt
- 1 tablespoon soy sauce
- 1 tablespoon sesame oil
- 4-5 green onions (scallions), cut into 2-inch pieces
- 100g (3.5 oz) mixed seafood (such as shrimp, squid, and/or mussels), chopped into small pieces
- Vegetable oil, for frying

Dipping Sauce:

- 2 tablespoons soy sauce
- 1 tablespoon rice vinegar or apple cider vinegar
- 1 teaspoon sesame oil
- 1/2 teaspoon sugar
- 1/2 teaspoon sesame seeds
- Optional: sliced fresh chili or chili flakes, to taste

Instructions:

1. **Prepare the batter:**
    - In a large bowl, whisk together flour, water, egg, salt, soy sauce, and sesame oil until smooth. The batter should have a pancake-like consistency. Let the batter rest for 10-15 minutes.
2. **Prepare the seafood and green onions:**
    - Heat a bit of vegetable oil in a skillet over medium-high heat. Stir-fry the mixed seafood for a few minutes until cooked through. Remove from heat and set aside.
    - Cut green onions into 2-inch pieces. You can use both the white and green parts of the green onions.
3. **Combine batter with seafood and green onions:**
    - Add cooked seafood and green onions to the batter. Gently fold them into the batter until evenly distributed.
4. **Cook the pancake:**
    - Heat a non-stick skillet or frying pan over medium heat. Add enough vegetable oil to coat the bottom of the pan.
    - Pour about half of the batter into the pan, spreading it out evenly to form a pancake about 1/2 inch thick.

- Cook for 3-4 minutes on each side, or until golden brown and crispy. Use a spatula to press down gently on the pancake while cooking to ensure it cooks evenly.
5. **Repeat with remaining batter:**
    - If needed, add more oil to the pan and repeat the process with the remaining batter to make another pancake.
6. **Make the dipping sauce:**
    - In a small bowl, mix together soy sauce, vinegar, sesame oil, sugar, sesame seeds, and chili (if using). Adjust seasoning to taste.
7. **Serve:**
    - Cut the Haemul Pajeon into wedges or squares and serve hot, with the dipping sauce on the side.

Haemul Pajeon is best enjoyed immediately while it's hot and crispy. It pairs wonderfully with the savory dipping sauce, adding an extra layer of flavor. This dish is perfect for sharing with family and friends as a delicious appetizer or side dish.

Bulgogi Jeongol (Beef and Vegetable Hot Pot)

Ingredients:

- 400g (14 oz) thinly sliced beef (such as sirloin or ribeye)
- 1 onion, thinly sliced
- 1 carrot, thinly sliced
- 1/2 small Napa cabbage, sliced
- 6-8 shiitake mushrooms, sliced
- 1 bunch enoki mushrooms (optional)
- 1 block firm tofu, cut into cubes
- 4 cups beef broth or water
- 2 tablespoons soy sauce
- 1 tablespoon sesame oil
- 1 tablespoon sugar
- 1 tablespoon mirin or rice wine
- 2 cloves garlic, minced
- 1 teaspoon black pepper
- 1 tablespoon vegetable oil
- Green onions, sliced (for garnish)
- Sesame seeds, for garnish

Dipping Sauce (optional):

- 2 tablespoons soy sauce
- 1 tablespoon rice vinegar or apple cider vinegar
- 1 teaspoon sesame oil
- 1/2 teaspoon sugar
- 1/2 teaspoon sesame seeds
- Optional: sliced fresh chili or chili flakes, to taste

Instructions:

1. **Marinate the beef:**
    - In a bowl, combine thinly sliced beef with soy sauce, sesame oil, sugar, mirin or rice wine, minced garlic, and black pepper. Mix well and let it marinate for at least 30 minutes in the refrigerator.
2. **Prepare the vegetables and tofu:**
    - Thinly slice onion, carrot, and Napa cabbage.
    - Slice shiitake mushrooms and trim enoki mushrooms.
    - Cut firm tofu into cubes.
3. **Cook Bulgogi Jeongol:**
    - Heat vegetable oil in a large pot or Korean hot pot (jeongol pan) over medium heat.

- Add marinated beef and stir-fry until it's browned and cooked through, about 3-4 minutes.
   - Add sliced onion, carrot, shiitake mushrooms, and Napa cabbage to the pot. Stir-fry for another 2-3 minutes until vegetables start to soften.
4. **Add broth and tofu:**
   - Pour beef broth or water into the pot. Bring to a boil, then reduce heat to medium-low.
   - Add cubed tofu to the pot and gently stir to combine with the beef and vegetables.
5. **Simmer and serve:**
   - Let Bulgogi Jeongol simmer for about 10-15 minutes, or until all ingredients are cooked through and flavors have melded together.
   - Taste and adjust seasoning with soy sauce or salt if needed.
6. **Prepare dipping sauce (optional):**
   - In a small bowl, mix together soy sauce, vinegar, sesame oil, sugar, sesame seeds, and chili (if using). Adjust seasoning to taste.
7. **Garnish and serve:**
   - Garnish Bulgogi Jeongol with sliced green onions and sesame seeds.
   - Serve hot directly from the pot, with dipping sauce on the side if desired.

Bulgogi Jeongol is a comforting and nutritious meal that's perfect for colder days or when you're craving a hearty Korean dish. Enjoy it with steamed rice and additional banchan (Korean side dishes) for a complete meal.

Dolsot Bibimbap (Stone Pot Mixed Rice)

Ingredients:

- 2 cups cooked short-grain rice (preferably Korean or sushi rice)
- 1 carrot, julienned
- 1 zucchini, julienned
- 1 cup spinach, blanched and squeezed dry
- 1 cup bean sprouts, blanched
- 150g (5 oz) beef (such as ribeye or sirloin), thinly sliced
- 4 shiitake mushrooms, thinly sliced
- 1 tablespoon vegetable oil
- 4 eggs
- Toasted sesame seeds, for garnish
- Thinly sliced green onions, for garnish
- Sesame oil, for drizzling

For the gochujang sauce:

- 4 tablespoons gochujang (Korean red chili paste)
- 2 tablespoons sesame oil
- 1 tablespoon soy sauce
- 1 tablespoon sugar
- 1 tablespoon water

Instructions:

1. **Prepare the vegetables:**
    - Julienne the carrot and zucchini into thin matchstick-sized pieces.
    - Blanch spinach in boiling water for about 30 seconds, then rinse with cold water and squeeze out excess water. Season lightly with salt and sesame oil.
    - Blanch bean sprouts in boiling water for about 1-2 minutes, then rinse with cold water and squeeze out excess water. Season lightly with salt and sesame oil.
2. **Cook the beef and mushrooms:**
    - Heat vegetable oil in a skillet over medium-high heat. Add sliced beef and shiitake mushrooms. Stir-fry until beef is cooked through and mushrooms are tender. Set aside.
3. **Prepare the gochujang sauce:**
    - In a small bowl, mix together gochujang, sesame oil, soy sauce, sugar, and water until smooth. Adjust seasoning to taste.
4. **Assemble Dolsot Bibimbap:**
    - Preheat a dolsot (stone pot) over medium heat until hot. Add a drizzle of sesame oil to coat the bottom and sides of the pot.

    - Spoon cooked rice into the dolsot, spreading it out evenly. Arrange cooked vegetables (carrot, zucchini, spinach, bean sprouts), beef, and mushrooms on top of the rice in separate sections.
5. **Cook the eggs:**
    - In a separate non-stick skillet, fry eggs sunny-side up or over-easy until the whites are set but the yolks are still runny.
6. **Serve:**
    - Carefully place fried eggs on top of the rice and vegetables in the dolsot.
    - Drizzle gochujang sauce over the ingredients.
    - Sprinkle toasted sesame seeds and thinly sliced green onions on top.
7. **Enjoy:**
    - Mix everything together thoroughly in the hot stone pot just before eating to combine all the flavors.
    - Serve hot, enjoying the crispy rice at the bottom of the pot.

Dolsot Bibimbap is a colorful and nutritious dish that's not only delicious but also visually appealing. It's a wonderful way to experience the vibrant flavors of Korean cuisine at home.

Mandu (Dumplings)

Ingredients:

For the filling:

- 250g (9 oz) ground pork or beef (or a combination)
- 1 cup firm tofu, drained and mashed
- 1 cup cabbage, finely chopped
- 1/2 cup carrot, finely chopped
- 3-4 shiitake mushrooms, finely chopped
- 2-3 green onions, finely chopped
- 2 cloves garlic, minced
- 1 tablespoon soy sauce
- 1 tablespoon sesame oil
- 1 teaspoon sugar
- 1/2 teaspoon black pepper
- 1/2 teaspoon salt, or to taste

For assembling:

- Round dumpling wrappers (mandu skins)
- Water, for sealing the wrappers

Dipping sauce:

- 2 tablespoons soy sauce
- 1 tablespoon rice vinegar or apple cider vinegar
- 1 teaspoon sesame oil
- 1 teaspoon sugar
- 1/2 teaspoon sesame seeds
- Optional: minced garlic, green onion, or chili flakes

Instructions:

1. **Prepare the filling:**
   - In a large bowl, combine ground pork or beef with mashed tofu, chopped cabbage, carrot, shiitake mushrooms, green onions, minced garlic, soy sauce, sesame oil, sugar, black pepper, and salt. Mix thoroughly until well combined.
2. **Assemble the mandu:**
   - Place a spoonful of filling in the center of a dumpling wrapper (about 1 tablespoon, depending on the size of your wrappers).
   - Dip your finger in water and moisten the edges of the wrapper.
   - Fold the wrapper over the filling to create a half-moon shape. Press the edges firmly to seal, making sure there are no air pockets. You can also pleat the edges for a decorative finish.

3. **Cook the mandu:**
   - **Boiling:** Bring a pot of water to a boil. Add mandu in batches (don't overcrowd the pot) and cook for about 5-7 minutes, or until they float to the surface and the filling is cooked through.
   - **Steaming:** Place mandu on a lightly greased steamer basket or steamer tray lined with parchment paper. Steam for about 10-12 minutes, or until cooked through.
   - **Pan-frying (Goon Mandu):** Heat a tablespoon of oil in a non-stick skillet over medium heat. Place mandu in the skillet in a single layer, leaving space between them. Fry for 2-3 minutes until the bottoms are golden brown. Add 1/4 cup of water to the skillet, cover with a lid, and cook for another 4-5 minutes, or until the water evaporates and the mandu are crispy on the bottom.
4. **Make the dipping sauce:**
   - In a small bowl, combine soy sauce, vinegar, sesame oil, sugar, sesame seeds, and any optional ingredients like minced garlic, green onion, or chili flakes. Mix well.
5. **Serve:**
   - Arrange mandu on a serving platter or individual plates.
   - Serve hot, accompanied by the dipping sauce.

Enjoy these homemade Korean mandu as a delicious appetizer, snack, or part of a meal. They're versatile and can be customized with various fillings and cooking methods to suit your taste preferences.

Hobakjuk (Pumpkin Porridge)

Ingredients:

- 1 cup peeled and diced pumpkin (butternut squash can also be used)
- 1/4 cup sweet rice flour (also known as glutinous rice flour)
- 4 cups water
- 1/4 cup sugar (adjust to taste)
- Pinch of salt
- Optional toppings: roasted pumpkin seeds, cinnamon powder

Instructions:

1. **Prepare the pumpkin:**
    - Peel the pumpkin and remove the seeds. Cut into small, evenly sized cubes.
2. **Cook the pumpkin:**
    - In a large pot, add the diced pumpkin and water. Bring to a boil over medium-high heat, then reduce the heat to medium-low and simmer for about 15-20 minutes, or until the pumpkin is tender and easily pierced with a fork.
3. **Blend the pumpkin:**
    - Using a blender or immersion blender, blend the cooked pumpkin until smooth. Alternatively, you can mash the pumpkin with a potato masher for a chunkier texture.
4. **Make the rice flour mixture:**
    - In a small bowl, mix the sweet rice flour with 1/2 cup of water until smooth and there are no lumps.
5. **Cook the porridge:**
    - Pour the rice flour mixture into the pot with the blended pumpkin. Stir well to combine.
    - Cook over medium-low heat, stirring constantly, for about 5-7 minutes until the porridge thickens to your desired consistency.
6. **Sweeten the porridge:**
    - Add sugar and a pinch of salt to the porridge, adjusting the sweetness according to your preference. Stir until the sugar is completely dissolved.
7. **Serve:**
    - Ladle the hot Hobakjuk into serving bowls.
    - Garnish with roasted pumpkin seeds and a sprinkle of cinnamon powder if desired.
8. **Enjoy:**
    - Serve warm as a comforting breakfast, snack, or dessert.

Hobakjuk can be served either warm or chilled, depending on your preference. It's a soothing dish that highlights the natural sweetness of pumpkin and is often enjoyed during Korean festive occasions or as a nourishing treat during colder seasons.

Doenjang Jjigae (Soybean Paste Stew)

Ingredients:

- 1/2 cup doenjang (Korean fermented soybean paste)
- 1 small onion, sliced
- 1 small zucchini, sliced
- 1 small potato, peeled and diced
- 1/2 cup tofu, diced
- 1 green chili pepper, sliced (optional)
- 2-3 cloves garlic, minced
- 4 cups water or anchovy stock (or vegetable broth for a vegetarian version)
- 1 tablespoon sesame oil
- 1 tablespoon vegetable oil
- 1 tablespoon gochujang (Korean red chili paste) (optional, for added spiciness)
- 1 tablespoon soy sauce (optional, for additional seasoning)
- 1 green onion, chopped (for garnish)
- Salt and pepper, to taste

Instructions:

1. **Prepare the vegetables:**
    - Slice the onion, zucchini, and green chili pepper (if using). Peel and dice the potato. Cut tofu into small cubes.
2. **Sauté the vegetables:**
    - Heat vegetable oil in a large pot or Korean earthenware pot (ttukbaegi) over medium heat. Add sliced onion and minced garlic. Sauté for 2-3 minutes until onions are translucent and garlic is fragrant.
3. **Add soybean paste and water/stock:**
    - Add doenjang (soybean paste) to the pot and stir well to combine with the onions and garlic. Cook for another minute.
    - Pour in water or anchovy stock (or vegetable broth). Bring to a boil, then reduce heat to medium-low and let it simmer for about 10 minutes to allow flavors to develop.
4. **Add remaining vegetables and tofu:**
    - Add sliced zucchini, diced potato, diced tofu, and sliced green chili pepper (if using) to the pot. Stir gently to mix with the stew.
5. **Season the stew:**
    - If using, add gochujang (Korean red chili paste) and soy sauce for additional flavor and spice. Stir well to incorporate.
    - Taste the stew and adjust seasoning with salt and pepper as needed. Be cautious with salt as doenjang is already salty.
6. **Simmer and serve:**
    - Continue to simmer the stew for another 10-15 minutes, or until the vegetables are tender and cooked through.

- Drizzle sesame oil over the stew and stir gently.
7. **Garnish and serve:**
    - Garnish with chopped green onion.
    - Serve hot, directly from the pot. Doenjang Jjigae is typically enjoyed with steamed rice and other Korean side dishes (banchan).

Doenjang Jjigae is a flavorful and nourishing dish that showcases the deep umami flavors of fermented soybean paste. It's a comforting stew that's perfect for warming up on chilly days and for sharing with family and friends.

Bossam (Boiled Pork Wraps)

Ingredients:

- 1 kg (2.2 lbs) pork belly
- 1/4 cup doenjang (Korean fermented soybean paste)
- 2 tablespoons gochujang (Korean red chili paste)
- 1 tablespoon soy sauce
- 1 tablespoon sesame oil
- 1 tablespoon rice wine or mirin
- 1 tablespoon sugar
- 6-8 cloves garlic, minced
- 1 onion, halved
- Fresh lettuce leaves, for wrapping
- Fresh perilla leaves (optional)
- Korean pickled radish (danmuji), thinly sliced
- Garlic cloves, thinly sliced
- Green chili peppers, thinly sliced (optional)
- Cooked white rice, for serving

Instructions:

1. **Prepare the pork belly:**
    - Place the pork belly in a large pot and cover with water. Add the halved onion and bring to a boil over high heat.
    - Reduce heat to medium-low and simmer for about 1.5 to 2 hours, or until the pork belly is tender and cooked through. Skim off any foam that rises to the surface.
    - Remove the pork belly from the pot and let it cool slightly. Slice into thin pieces.
2. **Prepare the seasoning sauce:**
    - In a bowl, combine doenjang (soybean paste), gochujang (red chili paste), soy sauce, sesame oil, rice wine or mirin, sugar, and minced garlic. Mix well to make a thick sauce.
3. **Serve Bossam:**
    - Arrange the sliced pork belly on a serving platter.
    - Serve with fresh lettuce leaves and perilla leaves (if using), Korean pickled radish, sliced garlic cloves, and green chili peppers.
4. **Wrap and enjoy:**
    - To enjoy Bossam, take a piece of lettuce or perilla leaf, add a slice of pork belly, a spoonful of the seasoning sauce, some sliced garlic, green chili peppers (if using), and a piece of pickled radish.
    - Wrap it up and eat it in one bite, combining the savory pork with the crunchy vegetables and tangy pickles.
    - Serve with steamed rice on the side.

Bossam is often enjoyed as a communal dish, where everyone wraps their own pieces according to their taste preferences. It's a flavorful and satisfying dish that highlights the balance of textures and flavors in Korean cuisine.

Gimbap (Korean Seaweed Rolls)

Ingredients:

- 4 cups cooked short-grain rice (preferably Korean or sushi rice)
- 5-6 sheets of dried seaweed (gim/nori)
- 1 tablespoon sesame oil
- 1 tablespoon sesame seeds
- Salt, to taste

For the filling (choose your favorites):

- 4-5 slices of ham or cooked spam, cut into strips
- 4-5 strips of imitation crab sticks
- 4-5 strips of cucumber, julienned
- 4-5 strips of carrots, julienned and blanched
- 4-5 strips of yellow pickled radish (danmuji)
- 4-5 strips of egg omelette, thinly sliced (seasoned with a pinch of salt and a bit of sugar)
- 4-5 spinach leaves, blanched and squeezed dry (optional)

Instructions:

1. **Prepare the rice:**
   - While the rice is still warm, transfer it to a large bowl. Drizzle sesame oil over the rice and sprinkle sesame seeds on top. Add salt to taste. Mix well until evenly seasoned. Let the rice cool slightly.
2. **Prepare the seaweed sheets (gim):**
   - Place a sheet of seaweed on a bamboo sushi mat or a clean kitchen towel. Spread a thin layer of seasoned rice evenly over the seaweed, leaving about 1 inch of seaweed at the top edge uncovered.
3. **Arrange the filling:**
   - Arrange the fillings in a line across the center of the rice-covered seaweed sheet, starting with your choice of ingredients. Be careful not to overfill.
4. **Roll the Gimbap:**
   - Lift the edge of the bamboo mat closest to you with your thumbs. Use your fingers to keep the fillings in place as you roll the mat away from you, enclosing the fillings in the rice-covered seaweed. Roll tightly but gently.
5. **Slice and serve:**
   - Once rolled, gently press the bamboo mat around the roll to secure it tightly.
   - With a sharp knife, slice the rolled Gimbap into bite-sized pieces, about 1 inch thick.
6. **Serve and enjoy:**
   - Arrange the sliced Gimbap on a serving plate. Serve with pickled radish (danmuji) and kimchi on the side.

- Gimbap can be enjoyed at room temperature or chilled. It's perfect for a light meal, lunchbox, or snack.

Tips:

- You can customize Gimbap with your favorite ingredients, such as tuna, bulgogi (marinated beef), avocado, or pickled vegetables.
- To prevent the rice from sticking to your hands, lightly moisten them with water or sesame oil when spreading the rice on the seaweed sheet.

Gimbap is not only delicious but also a fun dish to make with endless variations. It's a great way to explore Korean flavors and enjoy a satisfying meal on the go.

Yukgaejang (Spicy Beef Soup)

Ingredients:

- 300g (10.5 oz) beef brisket or flank steak, thinly sliced
- 1 onion, thinly sliced
- 1/2 cup fernbrake (gosari), soaked in water until softened
- 1/2 cup dried sliced shiitake mushrooms, soaked in water until softened
- 4-5 cups water
- 1 tablespoon sesame oil
- 2 tablespoons gochugaru (Korean red chili pepper flakes)
- 2 tablespoons soy sauce
- 1 tablespoon fish sauce
- 1 tablespoon minced garlic
- 1 teaspoon sesame seeds
- Salt and pepper, to taste
- 1 cup mung bean sprouts (optional)
- 2 green onions, chopped
- Cooked clear noodles (optional)

Instructions:

1. **Prepare the beef:**
   - In a large pot, add the beef slices and enough water to cover. Bring to a boil over medium-high heat, then reduce heat to low and simmer for about 20 minutes, skimming any foam that rises to the surface. Remove the beef from the pot and set aside.
2. **Prepare the vegetables:**
   - Drain and rinse the soaked fernbrake (gosari) and shiitake mushrooms. Cut gosari into bite-sized pieces if needed. Add them to the pot with 4-5 cups of fresh water.
3. **Make the broth:**
   - Add sliced onion, sesame oil, gochugaru (red chili pepper flakes), soy sauce, fish sauce, minced garlic, and sesame seeds to the pot. Stir well to combine.
   - Bring the mixture to a boil over medium-high heat. Reduce heat to low and simmer for about 30 minutes, or until the vegetables are tender and flavors have melded.
4. **Shred the beef:**
   - While the soup simmers, shred the cooked beef slices into thin strips using two forks or your fingers.
5. **Add shredded beef and optional ingredients:**
   - Add the shredded beef to the pot along with mung bean sprouts (if using). Simmer for an additional 10 minutes.
6. **Adjust seasoning and serve:**
   - Taste the soup and adjust seasoning with salt and pepper as needed.

- Stir in chopped green onions just before serving.
7. **Serve Yukgaejang:**
    - Ladle the hot Yukgaejang into serving bowls.
    - If using, add a portion of cooked clear noodles (optional) to each bowl.
    - Garnish with additional chopped green onions and serve hot.

Yukgaejang is best enjoyed hot and is often served with steamed rice and banchan (Korean side dishes). It's a comforting and nourishing soup that packs a spicy kick, perfect for warming up on cold days or for enjoying as a hearty meal any time of the year.

Ojingeo Bokkeum (Spicy Stir-Fried Squid)

Ingredients:

- 300g (10.5 oz) fresh squid, cleaned and cut into bite-sized pieces
- 1 small onion, thinly sliced
- 1/2 red bell pepper, thinly sliced
- 1/2 green bell pepper, thinly sliced
- 2-3 green onions, cut into 2-inch lengths
- 3-4 cloves garlic, minced
- 2 tablespoons vegetable oil
- 2 tablespoons gochugaru (Korean red chili pepper flakes)
- 1 tablespoon soy sauce
- 1 tablespoon mirin or rice wine
- 1 tablespoon honey or sugar
- 1 tablespoon sesame oil
- Sesame seeds, for garnish
- Salt and pepper, to taste

Instructions:

1. **Prepare the squid:**
   - Clean the squid thoroughly, removing any innards and cartilage. Cut into bite-sized pieces.
2. **Marinate the squid:**
   - In a bowl, combine the squid pieces with soy sauce, mirin (or rice wine), and a pinch of salt. Let it marinate for about 10-15 minutes.
3. **Stir-fry the vegetables:**
   - Heat vegetable oil in a large pan or wok over medium-high heat. Add minced garlic and stir-fry for about 30 seconds until fragrant.
   - Add sliced onion, red bell pepper, and green bell pepper. Stir-fry for 2-3 minutes until the vegetables start to soften.
4. **Cook the squid:**
   - Add the marinated squid to the pan. Stir-fry for another 3-4 minutes until the squid pieces are cooked through and opaque.
5. **Season the dish:**
   - Sprinkle gochugaru (Korean red chili pepper flakes) evenly over the squid and vegetables. Stir well to coat everything evenly.
   - Add honey (or sugar) and sesame oil. Mix thoroughly to combine and coat the ingredients with the sauce.
6. **Finish and garnish:**
   - Taste and adjust seasoning with salt and pepper if needed.
   - Stir in green onions and cook for another minute until they are slightly wilted.
   - Remove from heat and transfer to a serving plate.
7. **Serve Ojingeo Bokkeum:**

- - Garnish with sesame seeds.
  - Serve hot as a side dish (banchan) with steamed rice.

Ojingeo Bokkeum is spicy, savory, and slightly sweet, making it a delicious addition to any Korean meal. It's quick and easy to prepare, making it perfect for a weeknight dinner or as part of a Korean-inspired feast. Adjust the spiciness according to your preference by adding more or less gochugaru.

Banchan (Assorted Side Dishes)

Common Types of Banchan:

1. **Kimchi (Fermented Vegetables):**
    - **Napa Cabbage Kimchi:** Made with fermented cabbage, radish, and spicy seasoning.
    - **Baechu Kimchi:** Whole cabbage kimchi with a variety of seasonings.
    - **Oi Sobagi:** Stuffed cucumber kimchi.
2. **Namul (Seasoned Vegetables):**
    - **Sigeumchi Namul:** Seasoned spinach with sesame oil and garlic.
    - **Gaji Namul:** Seasoned eggplant.
    - **Kongnamul:** Seasoned soybean sprouts.
    - **Mu Sengchae:** Spicy radish salad.
3. **Jorim (Braised Dishes):**
    - **Gamja Jorim:** Braised potatoes in a soy sauce-based sauce.
    - **Jangjorim:** Beef strips braised in soy sauce and garlic.
4. **Jeon (Pan-fried Dishes):**
    - **Kimchi Jeon:** Pan-fried kimchi pancakes.
    - **Hobak Jeon:** Pan-fried zucchini slices in egg batter.
5. **Gyeran Mari (Rolled Omelette):**
    - **Gyeran Mari:** Rolled omelette with vegetables and sometimes seafood.
6. **Bokkeum (Stir-fried Dishes):**
    - **Ojingeo Bokkeum:** Spicy stir-fried squid.
    - **Gosari Namul Bokkeum:** Stir-fried fernbrake with soy sauce.
7. **Jjim (Steamed Dishes):**
    - **Gyeran Jjim:** Steamed egg custard.
8. **Fried Banchan:**
    - **Twigim:** Deep-fried vegetables or seafood.

Serving Banchan:

- Banchan dishes are typically served in small portions, meant to be shared family-style.
- A typical Korean meal includes a bowl of rice, soup (guk or jjigae), and an assortment of banchan.
- The variety of banchan can range from 3 to 12 dishes, depending on the occasion and formality of the meal.

Making Banchan:

- Banchan can be made ahead and stored in the refrigerator for several days.
- Each banchan dish has its own unique preparation method and ingredients, offering a diverse array of flavors and textures to complement the main dishes.

Enjoying Banchan:

- Banchan are meant to be enjoyed together with rice and other dishes, providing a balanced and satisfying meal.
- The combination of different flavors—spicy, salty, sweet, and sour—adds depth to the dining experience and enhances the enjoyment of Korean cuisine.

Banchan not only adds variety and nutrition to the meal but also reflects the rich culinary tradition and cultural heritage of Korean food.

Kongnamul Muchim (Seasoned Soybean Sprouts)

Ingredients:

- 400g (14 oz) soybean sprouts
- 2 cloves garlic, minced
- 1 green onion, finely chopped
- 1 tablespoon soy sauce
- 1 tablespoon sesame oil
- 1 tablespoon sesame seeds
- 1 teaspoon sugar (optional)
- 1 teaspoon gochugaru (Korean red chili pepper flakes), adjust to taste (optional)
- Salt, to taste

Instructions:

1. **Blanch the soybean sprouts:**
    - Bring a large pot of water to a boil. Add soybean sprouts and cook for about 1-2 minutes until they are tender but still crisp. Drain and rinse under cold water to stop the cooking process.
2. **Season the soybean sprouts:**
    - In a mixing bowl, combine the blanched soybean sprouts with minced garlic, chopped green onion, soy sauce, sesame oil, sesame seeds, sugar (if using), and gochugaru (if using).
    - Toss well to evenly coat the soybean sprouts with the seasoning. Adjust seasoning with salt if needed.
3. **Chill and serve:**
    - Refrigerate the seasoned soybean sprouts for at least 30 minutes to allow the flavors to meld.
    - Serve cold as a side dish (banchan) alongside rice and other Korean dishes.

Tips:

- **Blanching:** Be careful not to overcook the soybean sprouts; they should retain their crunchiness.
- **Adjusting Spiciness:** Gochugaru adds a mild spiciness and vibrant color to the dish. Adjust the amount according to your preference.
- **Storage:** Leftover Kongnamul Muchim can be stored in an airtight container in the refrigerator for up to 2-3 days.

Kongnamul Muchim is a versatile banchan that complements a wide range of Korean meals. Its fresh, crisp texture and savory-sweet flavor make it a favorite among both adults and children. Enjoy this dish as part of a Korean meal or as a healthy snack!

Jeyuk Bokkeum (Spicy Stir-Fried Pork)

Ingredients:

- 500g (1.1 lbs) pork shoulder or belly, thinly sliced
- 1 onion, thinly sliced
- 1 carrot, julienned
- 4-5 green onions, cut into 2-inch lengths
- 4-5 cloves garlic, minced
- 2 tablespoons vegetable oil
- Sesame seeds, for garnish

For the marinade:

- 3 tablespoons gochujang (Korean red chili pepper paste)
- 2 tablespoons soy sauce
- 1 tablespoon gochugaru (Korean red chili pepper flakes)
- 1 tablespoon honey or sugar
- 1 tablespoon sesame oil
- 1 tablespoon rice wine or mirin
- 1 teaspoon minced ginger
- 1/2 teaspoon black pepper

Instructions:

1. **Marinate the pork:**
    - In a bowl, combine all the marinade ingredients: gochujang, soy sauce, gochugaru, honey (or sugar), sesame oil, rice wine (or mirin), minced ginger, and black pepper.
    - Add the thinly sliced pork to the marinade and mix well to coat. Let it marinate for at least 30 minutes to allow the flavors to absorb.
2. **Prepare the vegetables:**
    - Heat vegetable oil in a large pan or wok over medium-high heat. Add minced garlic and stir-fry for about 30 seconds until fragrant.
    - Add sliced onion and julienned carrot. Stir-fry for 2-3 minutes until the vegetables start to soften.
3. **Cook the pork:**
    - Add the marinated pork to the pan. Stir-fry for 5-6 minutes until the pork is cooked through and caramelized, and the sauce has thickened.
4. **Add green onions:**
    - Stir in the green onions and cook for another 1-2 minutes until they are slightly wilted.
5. **Garnish and serve:**
    - Transfer the Jeyuk Bokkeum to a serving plate. Sprinkle sesame seeds on top for garnish.

6. **Serve Jeyuk Bokkeum:**
   - Serve hot with steamed rice and other Korean banchan (side dishes) such as kimchi, namul, or pickled vegetables.

Tips:

- **Adjusting Spiciness:** You can adjust the spiciness of Jeyuk Bokkeum by varying the amount of gochugaru (red chili pepper flakes) and gochujang (red chili pepper paste) according to your taste preference.
- **Serving Suggestions:** Jeyuk Bokkeum pairs well with fresh lettuce leaves for wrapping, along with a dollop of ssamjang (seasoned soybean paste).

Jeyuk Bokkeum is a flavorful and satisfying dish that showcases the spicy and savory flavors characteristic of Korean cuisine. Enjoy this dish as a main course or as part of a Korean-inspired meal!

Gochujang Samgyeopsal (Grilled Pork Belly with Chili Paste)

Ingredients:

- 500g (1.1 lbs) pork belly, thinly sliced
- 3 tablespoons gochujang (Korean red chili paste)
- 2 tablespoons soy sauce
- 2 tablespoons honey or sugar
- 1 tablespoon sesame oil
- 4-5 cloves garlic, minced
- 1 tablespoon sesame seeds
- Fresh lettuce leaves, for serving
- Ssamjang (seasoned soybean paste), for serving (optional)
- Sliced garlic cloves, for serving (optional)
- Sliced green onions, for garnish (optional)

Instructions:

1. **Prepare the marinade:**
    - In a bowl, combine gochujang, soy sauce, honey (or sugar), sesame oil, minced garlic, and sesame seeds. Mix well until the ingredients are evenly combined.
2. **Marinate the pork belly:**
    - Place the thinly sliced pork belly in a large bowl or resealable plastic bag. Pour the marinade over the pork, making sure each slice is coated evenly. Marinate for at least 30 minutes to 1 hour in the refrigerator.
3. **Grill the pork belly:**
    - Heat a grill or a grill pan over medium-high heat.
    - Grill the marinated pork belly slices for about 2-3 minutes on each side, or until they are cooked through and caramelized. Pork belly cooks quickly due to its thinness, so keep an eye on it to prevent overcooking.
4. **Serve Gochujang Samgyeopsal:**
    - Arrange the grilled pork belly slices on a serving plate.
    - Serve with fresh lettuce leaves for wrapping the pork, along with sliced garlic, ssamjang (if using), and sliced green onions for garnish.
    - Optionally, provide a bowl of steamed rice to enjoy with the lettuce wraps.
5. **Enjoy:**
    - To eat, place a piece of grilled pork belly in a lettuce leaf, add a small amount of ssamjang and sliced garlic (if desired), wrap it up, and enjoy!

Tips:

- **Grilling:** If you don't have a grill, you can also cook the pork belly in a skillet or grill pan on the stovetop.
- **Adjusting Spiciness:** You can adjust the spiciness of the marinade by adding more or less gochujang according to your preference.

- **Variations:** Feel free to add other banchan (side dishes) such as kimchi, pickled vegetables, or namul (seasoned vegetables) to complement the meal.

Gochujang Samgyeopsal is a flavorful and satisfying dish that's perfect for a Korean BBQ experience at home. It's great for sharing with family and friends, and the combination of spicy gochujang and tender pork belly is sure to be a hit!

Eomuk Bokkeum (Stir-Fried Fish Cake)

Ingredients:

- 300g (10.5 oz) eomuk (fish cakes), thinly sliced
- 1/2 onion, thinly sliced
- 1/2 carrot, julienned
- 1/2 red bell pepper, thinly sliced
- 2-3 green onions, cut into 2-inch lengths
- 2 cloves garlic, minced
- 1 tablespoon vegetable oil
- Sesame seeds, for garnish

For the sauce:

- 2 tablespoons soy sauce
- 1 tablespoon gochujang (Korean red chili pepper paste)
- 1 tablespoon honey or sugar
- 1 tablespoon sesame oil
- 1 teaspoon minced ginger
- 1/2 cup water

Instructions:

1. **Prepare the sauce:**
    - In a bowl, combine soy sauce, gochujang, honey (or sugar), sesame oil, minced ginger, and water. Mix well until smooth and set aside.
2. **Stir-fry the vegetables and fish cakes:**
    - Heat vegetable oil in a large pan or wok over medium-high heat.
    - Add minced garlic and stir-fry for about 30 seconds until fragrant.
    - Add sliced onion, julienned carrot, and red bell pepper. Stir-fry for 2-3 minutes until the vegetables start to soften.
3. **Add fish cakes and sauce:**
    - Add the thinly sliced fish cakes (eomuk) to the pan.
    - Pour the prepared sauce over the fish cakes and vegetables. Stir well to coat everything evenly.
4. **Simmer and finish:**
    - Bring the mixture to a simmer. Cook for 3-4 minutes, stirring occasionally, until the sauce thickens slightly and the fish cakes are heated through.
5. **Garnish and serve:**
    - Sprinkle sesame seeds over the Eomuk Bokkeum for garnish.
    - Serve hot as a side dish (banchan) alongside steamed rice.

Tips:

- **Fish Cakes (Eomuk):** You can find eomuk (fish cakes) in Asian grocery stores. They come in various shapes and sizes, so you can choose your favorite type for this dish.
- **Adjusting Spiciness:** If you prefer a spicier dish, you can add more gochujang or a dash of gochugaru (Korean red chili pepper flakes) to the sauce.
- **Variations:** Feel free to add other vegetables such as mushrooms, zucchini, or spinach to enhance the dish.

Eomuk Bokkeum is a flavorful and versatile dish that's quick to prepare and perfect for adding variety to a Korean meal. Enjoy its savory-sweet flavors and tender texture as part of your next Korean-inspired dining experience!

Gyeran Jjim (Steamed Egg)

Ingredients:

- 3 large eggs
- 1/2 cup water or chicken broth
- 1/2 teaspoon salt
- 1 teaspoon soy sauce
- 1/2 teaspoon sesame oil
- 1 green onion, finely chopped (optional)
- Sesame seeds, for garnish
- Thinly sliced green onion, for garnish

Instructions:

1. **Prepare the egg mixture:**
     - In a mixing bowl, crack the eggs and beat them gently with a fork or whisk.
     - Add water or chicken broth, salt, soy sauce, sesame oil, and chopped green onion (if using). Mix well until everything is combined.
2. **Steam the eggs:**
     - Lightly grease a heatproof dish or a steaming bowl that fits into your steamer. You can use a ceramic dish or any heatproof bowl.
     - Pour the egg mixture into the dish or bowl.
3. **Steam the eggs:**
     - Heat water in a steamer over medium-high heat until it comes to a boil.
     - Place the dish with the egg mixture into the steamer basket. Cover with a lid and steam over medium heat for about 10-12 minutes, or until the eggs are set and slightly puffed.
4. **Garnish and serve:**
     - Carefully remove the dish from the steamer. The Gyeran Jjim should be firm but still silky and custard-like.
     - Garnish with sesame seeds and thinly sliced green onion on top for added flavor and presentation.
5. **Serve Gyeran Jjim:**
     - Serve hot as a side dish (banchan) alongside steamed rice and other Korean dishes.

Tips:

- **Consistency:** The texture of Gyeran Jjim should be smooth and custard-like. Adjust the steaming time accordingly to achieve the desired consistency.
- **Variations:** You can customize Gyeran Jjim by adding other ingredients such as minced vegetables, seafood, or even kimchi for extra flavor.

- **Steaming:** If you don't have a steamer, you can improvise by using a large pot with a lid and placing a heatproof dish or bowl inside, elevated with a trivet or overturned heatproof bowl to allow steam circulation.

Gyeran Jjim is a comforting and versatile dish that's enjoyed by both adults and children alike in Korean cuisine. Its simplicity in preparation and delicate taste make it a perfect addition to any Korean meal!

Kimchi Fried Rice

Ingredients:

- 2 cups cooked rice (preferably day-old rice)
- 1 cup kimchi, chopped
- 1/2 cup kimchi juice (from the kimchi jar)
- 150g (5 oz) pork belly or bacon, diced (optional)
- 1/2 onion, finely chopped
- 2 cloves garlic, minced
- 1 tablespoon vegetable oil
- 1 tablespoon soy sauce
- 1 tablespoon gochujang (Korean red chili pepper paste), optional for added spice
- 1 teaspoon sesame oil
- 2 green onions, chopped (separate white and green parts)
- Sesame seeds, for garnish
- Fried eggs, for serving (optional)

Instructions:

1. **Prepare the ingredients:**
   - If using pork belly or bacon, dice it into small pieces. Chop the kimchi into bite-sized pieces and reserve the kimchi juice.
   - Finely chop the onion, mince the garlic, and chop the green onions, separating the white and green parts.
2. **Cook the pork belly (optional):**
   - Heat a large pan or wok over medium-high heat. Add the diced pork belly or bacon and cook until browned and crispy. Remove excess fat if desired.
3. **Stir-fry the vegetables:**
   - In the same pan, add vegetable oil and heat over medium heat. Add the chopped onion and white parts of the green onions. Stir-fry for 2-3 minutes until softened.
4. **Add kimchi and garlic:**
   - Add the chopped kimchi and minced garlic to the pan. Stir-fry for another 2-3 minutes until the kimchi is slightly caramelized and aromatic.
5. **Add rice and seasonings:**
   - Add the cooked rice to the pan. Break up any clumps of rice with a spatula.
   - Pour in the kimchi juice and soy sauce. If using gochujang, add it now for added spice. Stir-fry everything together for 5-6 minutes until the rice is well coated and heated through.
6. **Finish and garnish:**
   - Drizzle sesame oil over the fried rice and toss to combine.
   - Garnish with chopped green onions (green parts) and sesame seeds.
7. **Serve Kimchi Fried Rice:**
   - Serve hot, optionally topped with a fried egg or any other protein of your choice.

Tips:

- **Rice:** Day-old rice works best for fried rice as it is drier and less sticky. Freshly cooked rice can be spread out on a tray and cooled in the refrigerator for 1-2 hours before using.
- **Customization:** You can add other ingredients like vegetables (bell peppers, peas, carrots), tofu, or shrimp to suit your taste.
- **Spiciness:** Adjust the amount of gochujang or kimchi juice based on your preference for spiciness.

Kimchi Fried Rice is a versatile dish that's perfect for a quick meal or as part of a Korean-inspired feast. It's packed with umami flavors from the kimchi and makes a satisfying meal any time of day!

Dakkochi (Grilled Chicken Skewers)

Ingredients:

- 500g (1.1 lbs) boneless, skinless chicken thighs or breasts, cut into bite-sized pieces
- 10-12 wooden skewers, soaked in water for 30 minutes
- 2 tablespoons soy sauce
- 2 tablespoons honey or brown sugar
- 1 tablespoon gochujang (Korean red chili pepper paste)
- 1 tablespoon mirin or rice wine
- 1 tablespoon sesame oil
- 2 cloves garlic, minced
- 1 teaspoon grated ginger
- 1 green onion, finely chopped
- Sesame seeds, for garnish
- Vegetable oil, for grilling

Instructions:

1. **Prepare the marinade:**
   - In a bowl, combine soy sauce, honey or brown sugar, gochujang, mirin or rice wine, sesame oil, minced garlic, grated ginger, and chopped green onion. Mix well until smooth.
2. **Marinate the chicken:**
   - Add the chicken pieces to the marinade and toss to coat evenly. Cover and refrigerate for at least 1 hour, or overnight for best flavor.
3. **Skewer the chicken:**
   - Thread the marinated chicken pieces onto the soaked wooden skewers, dividing them evenly.
4. **Grill the Dakkochi:**
   - Preheat a grill or grill pan over medium-high heat. Lightly brush the grill with vegetable oil to prevent sticking.
   - Place the skewers on the grill and cook for 3-4 minutes on each side, or until the chicken is cooked through and has grill marks. Baste with any remaining marinade while grilling.
5. **Garnish and serve:**
   - Remove the Dakkochi from the grill and transfer to a serving platter.
   - Sprinkle sesame seeds over the skewers for garnish.
   - Serve hot as an appetizer or snack, optionally with a side of dipping sauce such as ssamjang (seasoned soybean paste).

Tips:

- **Alternative Cooking Methods:** If you don't have a grill, you can cook Dakkochi in a grill pan on the stovetop or under the broiler in the oven.

- **Dipping Sauce:** Dakkochi pairs well with a dipping sauce made from soy sauce, vinegar, and a dash of sesame oil, or simply with ssamjang for extra flavor.
- **Variations:** You can add vegetables like bell peppers, onions, or mushrooms between the chicken pieces on the skewers for added flavor and texture.

Dakkochi is a delicious and easy-to-make Korean dish that's perfect for gatherings or as a quick snack. Enjoy the sweet and savory flavors of these grilled chicken skewers with your favorite sides!

Jajangmyeon (Noodles in Black Bean Sauce)

Ingredients:

- 300g (10.5 oz) fresh or dried Korean-style wheat noodles (or substitute with udon noodles)
- 150g (5 oz) pork belly or pork shoulder, diced into small pieces
- 1 large onion, finely diced
- 1 medium zucchini, diced
- 1 large potato, diced
- 1/2 cup black bean paste (chunjang or Korean jjajang)
- 1 tablespoon vegetable oil
- 1 tablespoon sesame oil
- 1 tablespoon soy sauce
- 1 tablespoon sugar
- 1 cup water or chicken broth
- 2 cloves garlic, minced
- 1 tablespoon cornstarch mixed with 2 tablespoons water (optional, for thickening)
- Fresh cucumber strips, for garnish (optional)
- Pickled radish (danmuji), for serving (optional)

Instructions:

1. **Prepare the noodles:**
   - Cook the noodles according to the package instructions until al dente. Drain and rinse under cold water to prevent sticking. Set aside.
2. **Prepare the sauce:**
   - In a small bowl, mix together the black bean paste (chunjang), soy sauce, and sugar. Set aside.
3. **Cook the pork and vegetables:**
   - Heat vegetable oil in a large pan or wok over medium-high heat. Add the diced pork and cook until browned and crispy.
   - Add minced garlic, diced onion, zucchini, and potato to the pan. Stir-fry for 3-4 minutes until the vegetables begin to soften.
4. **Add the black bean sauce:**
   - Push the pork and vegetables to the side of the pan. Add the black bean paste mixture to the center of the pan. Stir-fry the paste for about 1 minute to release its flavors.
5. **Combine and simmer:**
   - Mix the pork, vegetables, and black bean sauce together in the pan until everything is well coated.
   - Pour in water or chicken broth. Bring the mixture to a boil, then reduce the heat to medium-low and let it simmer for about 10-15 minutes, or until the sauce has thickened and the vegetables are tender. If desired, you can add the cornstarch slurry (cornstarch mixed with water) to thicken the sauce further.

6. **Serve Jajangmyeon:**
    - Divide the cooked noodles among serving bowls.
    - Ladle the hot black bean sauce over the noodles.
    - Garnish with fresh cucumber strips and serve with pickled radish (danmuji) on the side, if desired.

Tips:

- **Vegetarian Option:** You can omit the pork and add more vegetables or tofu for a vegetarian version of Jajangmyeon.
- **Noodle Substitution:** If you can't find Korean-style wheat noodles, you can use udon noodles or even spaghetti as a substitute.
- **Adjusting Consistency:** If the sauce becomes too thick during cooking, you can add more water or broth to adjust the consistency.

Jajangmyeon is a comforting and flavorful dish that's popular in Korean cuisine. It's enjoyed by families and as a quick meal option, offering a unique blend of savory and slightly sweet flavors from the black bean sauce. Enjoy making and savoring this Korean-Chinese classic at home!

Budae Jjigae (Army Stew)

Ingredients:

- 200g (7 oz) sliced pork belly or shoulder
- 1/2 onion, thinly sliced
- 1/2 cup kimchi, chopped
- 1/2 cup kimchi juice (from the kimchi jar)
- 1 cup sliced sausage (e.g., hot dogs, Vienna sausages)
- 1 cup spam, sliced into cubes
- 1 cup tofu, cubed
- 1 cup sliced mushrooms (button mushrooms or shiitake mushrooms)
- 1 cup sliced rice cakes (tteok)
- 2 cups napa cabbage, chopped
- 4 cups water or chicken broth
- 2 tablespoons gochujang (Korean red chili pepper paste)
- 1 tablespoon gochugaru (Korean red chili pepper flakes)
- 2 tablespoons soy sauce
- 1 tablespoon minced garlic
- 1 tablespoon sesame oil
- 1 tablespoon vegetable oil
- 2 green onions, chopped (separate white and green parts)
- 1 pack instant ramen noodles (optional)
- Salt and pepper, to taste

Instructions:

1. **Prepare the ingredients:**
   - Heat vegetable oil in a large pot or deep skillet over medium-high heat. Add sliced pork and cook until browned.
   - Add minced garlic and sliced onions. Stir-fry for about 2 minutes until onions are translucent.
2. **Add kimchi and seasoning:**
   - Add chopped kimchi, kimchi juice, gochujang, gochugaru, soy sauce, and sesame oil to the pot. Stir well to combine and cook for another 3-4 minutes.
3. **Add sausage, spam, and vegetables:**
   - Add sliced sausage, cubed spam, tofu, mushrooms, sliced rice cakes, and chopped napa cabbage to the pot. Stir to combine everything evenly.
4. **Simmer the stew:**
   - Pour water or chicken broth into the pot. Bring the stew to a boil, then reduce heat to medium-low. Cover and simmer for 15-20 minutes, or until the vegetables are tender and the flavors have melded together.
5. **Adjust seasoning and add noodles (optional):**
   - Taste and adjust the seasoning with salt and pepper if needed.

- If using instant ramen noodles, break them into pieces and add them to the stew. Cook for an additional 3-4 minutes until the noodles are cooked through.
6. **Finish and serve Budae Jjigae:**
    - Garnish with chopped green onions (green parts).
    - Serve hot directly from the pot or transfer to a serving bowl.

Tips:

- **Variations:** Budae Jjigae is very versatile, and you can adjust the ingredients based on what you have or prefer. Feel free to add other ingredients like baked beans, cheese slices, or vegetables such as spinach or enoki mushrooms.
- **Spiciness:** Adjust the amount of gochujang and gochugaru according to your spice preference. You can make it milder or spicier by adding more or less.
- **Storage:** Budae Jjigae can be stored in the refrigerator for up to 3 days. The flavors often deepen and improve after sitting overnight.

Budae Jjigae is a comforting and flavorful stew that's perfect for sharing with family and friends. Its unique blend of Korean and American ingredients makes it a nostalgic and satisfying dish that's enjoyed across generations.

Sannakji (Live Octopus)

Ingredients:

- Live octopus (small octopus or baby octopus)
- Sesame oil
- Sesame seeds (optional)
- Soy sauce (optional, for dipping)

Instructions:

1. **Preparation:**
   - It's crucial to start with very fresh octopus. The octopus is typically killed just before serving, or in some cases, served alive.
   - To prepare, the octopus is cleaned thoroughly to remove any dirt or residue. It's then cut into small pieces, often bite-sized.
2. **Serving:**
   - Sannakji is served immediately after preparation to emphasize its freshness and tenderness. The pieces of octopus may still be moving or squirming slightly due to residual nerve activity.
   - The octopus pieces are arranged on a plate and drizzled with sesame oil. Some versions may sprinkle sesame seeds over the top for added flavor and texture.
3. **Eating:**
   - To eat Sannakji, take a piece of octopus with chopsticks. It's common to chew carefully as the suction cups may stick to the inside of the mouth or throat due to their suction properties.
   - It's often enjoyed with a side of soy sauce mixed with wasabi or gochujang (Korean chili paste) for dipping, though purists may prefer to taste the natural flavors of the octopus with just sesame oil.

Safety Note:

- Eating live octopus (Sannakji) requires caution due to the risk of choking. It's important to chew thoroughly and carefully to avoid any suction cups sticking to the throat.

Cultural Context:

- Sannakji is more than just a dish; it's an experience that highlights the freshness and unique texture of octopus. It's often enjoyed as a novelty or delicacy in Korean cuisine, particularly in coastal regions where seafood is abundant.

Sannakji is not for everyone due to its unique preparation and texture, but for those who enjoy seafood and are looking for a memorable culinary experience, it can be an adventurous dish to try.

Kalguksu (Handmade Noodle Soup)

Ingredients:

For the noodle dough:

- 2 cups all-purpose flour
- 1/2 teaspoon salt
- 1/2 cup water

For the soup:

- 6 cups chicken broth or anchovy broth (or a combination)
- 1 cup diced chicken breast or thigh meat (optional)
- 1/2 onion, thinly sliced
- 2 cloves garlic, minced
- 1 tablespoon soy sauce
- 1 tablespoon sesame oil
- Salt and pepper, to taste

Optional toppings:

- Thinly sliced zucchini
- Thinly sliced carrots
- Sliced mushrooms (shiitake or button mushrooms)
- Thinly sliced green onions
- Fried tofu (dubu) cubes
- Sesame seeds, for garnish
- Kimchi, for serving (optional)

Instructions:

1. **Make the noodle dough:**
   - In a large bowl, combine the flour and salt. Gradually add water, stirring with a fork or your hands, until the mixture comes together into a dough.
   - Knead the dough on a lightly floured surface for about 5-7 minutes until smooth and elastic. Cover with a damp cloth and let it rest for at least 30 minutes.
2. **Prepare the soup base:**
   - In a large pot, heat sesame oil over medium heat. Add minced garlic and sauté until fragrant.
   - Add diced chicken (if using) and cook until lightly browned.
   - Add sliced onions and continue to cook until onions are softened.
3. **Add broth and seasonings:**
   - Pour in chicken broth or anchovy broth (or a combination of both). Bring to a boil, then reduce heat to medium-low and simmer for about 10-15 minutes to develop flavors.

- Season with soy sauce, salt, and pepper to taste. Adjust seasoning as needed.
4. **Roll out and cut the noodles:**
    - Divide the rested dough into two portions. Roll out each portion thinly on a floured surface using a rolling pin.
    - Cut the rolled-out dough into thin strips with a sharp knife to form noodles. Dust with flour to prevent sticking.
5. **Cook the noodles and assemble:**
    - Bring a large pot of water to a boil. Add the freshly cut noodles and cook for about 3-5 minutes, or until they float to the surface and are tender but still chewy.
    - Drain the noodles and rinse briefly under cold water to remove excess starch.
6. **Serve Kalguksu:**
    - Divide the cooked noodles into serving bowls.
    - Ladle the hot soup over the noodles. Top with any optional toppings such as sliced vegetables, tofu cubes, green onions, and sesame seeds.
    - Serve hot with kimchi on the side, if desired.

Tips:

- **Broth Options:** You can use chicken broth, anchovy broth, or a combination of both for the soup base. Anchovy broth adds a deep umami flavor, while chicken broth provides a richer taste.
- **Noodle Consistency:** For best results, roll the dough thinly and cut the noodles into uniform strips. This ensures they cook evenly and have a pleasing texture.
- **Customization:** Feel free to add or substitute toppings based on your preference or what you have on hand. Kalguksu is versatile and can accommodate a variety of vegetables and proteins.

Kalguksu is a comforting and versatile dish that's perfect for warming up during chilly days. Enjoy the handmade noodles and flavorful broth in this classic Korean soup!

Ssambap (Lettuce Wraps with Rice)

Ingredients:

- Cooked rice (white rice or mixed grain rice)
- Lettuce leaves (such as green leaf lettuce or romaine lettuce), washed and dried
- Thinly sliced vegetables:
    - Cucumber
    - Carrots
    - Radish
    - Bell peppers
- Protein options (choose one or more):
    - Grilled beef bulgogi
    - Grilled chicken
    - Pan-fried tofu
    - Sliced cooked egg
- Kimchi, for serving (optional)
- Sesame seeds, for garnish

Sauce:

- 2 tablespoons gochujang (Korean red chili pepper paste)
- 1 tablespoon sesame oil
- 1 tablespoon soy sauce
- 1 tablespoon honey or sugar
- 1 clove garlic, minced
- 1 teaspoon sesame seeds
- 1 green onion, finely chopped

Instructions:

1. **Prepare the sauce:**
    - In a small bowl, combine gochujang, sesame oil, soy sauce, honey or sugar, minced garlic, sesame seeds, and chopped green onion. Mix well until smooth. Adjust sweetness and spiciness to taste by adding more honey or gochujang if desired.
2. **Prepare the ingredients:**
    - Cook rice according to package instructions and keep warm.
    - Prepare the vegetables by slicing them thinly. You can lightly pickle them in vinegar for extra flavor if desired.
    - Cook or prepare your protein of choice (grilled bulgogi, chicken, tofu, or egg) and slice thinly for easy wrapping.
3. **Assemble Ssambap:**
    - Place a lettuce leaf on a plate. Add a spoonful of cooked rice in the center of the leaf.

- Layer with slices of your chosen protein and assorted vegetables on top of the rice.
4. **Wrap and serve:**
   - Drizzle a small amount of the prepared sauce over the filling.
   - Fold the lettuce leaf over the filling and roll it up like a burrito, securing with your hands or a toothpick if needed.
   - Repeat with the remaining ingredients to make more wraps.
5. **Serve Ssambap:**
   - Arrange the wrapped Ssambap on a platter or individual plates.
   - Serve with extra sauce on the side for dipping and kimchi for additional flavor.
   - Sprinkle sesame seeds over the wraps for garnish.

Tips:

- **Variations:** Feel free to customize Ssambap with your favorite vegetables, proteins, or sauces. You can also add fresh herbs like mint or cilantro for extra freshness.
- **Make it Vegan:** Opt for tofu or vegetable-based proteins and ensure the sauce is vegan-friendly by using vegan gochujang and soy sauce.
- **Eating:** Ssambap is meant to be eaten by hand. Dip each bite into the sauce before enjoying it for a burst of flavor.

Ssambap is a delightful and healthy Korean dish that allows you to enjoy different textures and flavors in each bite. It's perfect for gatherings or a satisfying meal at home, offering a balance of rice, vegetables, protein, and a touch of spicy-sweet sauce.

Hotteok (Sweet Stuffed Pancakes)

Ingredients:

For the dough:

- 1 cup all-purpose flour
- 1/2 cup lukewarm water
- 1 tablespoon sugar
- 1/2 teaspoon active dry yeast
- Pinch of salt

For the filling:

- 1/2 cup brown sugar
- 1/2 cup chopped mixed nuts (such as peanuts, walnuts, or almonds)
- 1 tablespoon honey
- 1/2 teaspoon cinnamon powder

Additional ingredients:

- Vegetable oil, for cooking

Instructions:

1. **Prepare the dough:**
    - In a mixing bowl, combine lukewarm water, sugar, and active dry yeast. Let it sit for 5-10 minutes until frothy.
    - Add flour and a pinch of salt to the yeast mixture. Mix well until it forms a dough.
    - Knead the dough for about 5-7 minutes until smooth and elastic. Cover with a damp cloth and let it rest in a warm place for about 1 hour, or until it doubles in size.
2. **Make the filling:**
    - In a separate bowl, mix together brown sugar, chopped nuts, honey, and cinnamon powder until well combined. Set aside.
3. **Shape the Hotteok:**
    - After the dough has risen, divide it into equal-sized balls (about the size of golf balls).
    - Flatten each ball with your hands to form a small disc. Place a spoonful of the filling (about 1-2 tablespoons) in the center of the disc.
4. **Seal and shape the Hotteok:**
    - Gather the edges of the dough disc together to seal the filling inside, pinching it closed at the top.
    - Gently flatten the filled dough ball with your palms to form a pancake shape, about 1/2 inch thick.
5. **Cook the Hotteok:**

- Heat a non-stick skillet or griddle over medium heat. Add a generous amount of vegetable oil.
- Place the stuffed pancakes on the skillet, seam side down. Press gently with a spatula to flatten slightly.
- Cook for about 2-3 minutes on each side, or until golden brown and crispy.

6. **Serve Hotteok:**
   - Remove the cooked Hotteok from the skillet and drain excess oil on paper towels.
   - Serve hot and crispy. Enjoy them as a snack or dessert.

Tips:

- **Variations:** You can customize the filling by adding ingredients like sweetened red bean paste, cheese, or even Nutella for a different twist.
- **Storage:** Hotteok is best enjoyed fresh and hot off the skillet. However, you can store any leftover Hotteok in an airtight container at room temperature and reheat in a toaster oven for a few minutes before serving.

Hotteok is a delightful treat that's enjoyed year-round in Korea, especially during colder months. Its crispy exterior and sweet, nutty filling make it a favorite street food among locals and visitors alike. Enjoy making and savoring these sweet stuffed pancakes at home!

Gamjatang (Spicy Pork Bone Soup)

Ingredients:

- 2 lbs pork neck bones or pork spine bones, cut into pieces
- 1 onion, quartered
- 6 cloves garlic, minced
- 2-inch piece ginger, sliced
- 8 cups water
- 1 tablespoon doenjang (Korean fermented soybean paste)
- 1 tablespoon gochugaru (Korean red chili pepper flakes)
- 1 tablespoon gochujang (Korean red chili pepper paste)
- 1 tablespoon soy sauce
- 1 tablespoon sesame oil
- 1 tablespoon fish sauce (optional, for extra umami)
- 1 teaspoon ground black pepper
- 2 potatoes, peeled and cut into chunks
- 1 zucchini, sliced
- 1 bunch of green onions, cut into 2-inch pieces
- 1 cup chopped kimchi (optional, for added flavor)
- Salt, to taste
- Sesame seeds and sliced green onions for garnish

Instructions:

1. **Prepare the pork bones:**
   - Rinse the pork bones under cold water to remove any blood or bone fragments.
   - In a large pot, add the pork bones, onion, garlic, and ginger slices. Cover with water and bring to a boil over high heat.
2. **Boil and skim:**
   - Once boiling, reduce heat to medium-low and simmer for 20 minutes. Skim off any foam or impurities that rise to the surface.
3. **Add seasonings:**
   - Add doenjang, gochugaru, gochujang, soy sauce, sesame oil, fish sauce (if using), and black pepper. Stir well to combine and dissolve the doenjang and gochujang.
4. **Simmer the broth:**
   - Cover the pot and simmer over low heat for 1.5 to 2 hours, or until the pork bones are tender and the broth is rich and flavorful.
5. **Add vegetables:**
   - Add potatoes, zucchini, green onions, and kimchi (if using) to the pot. Continue to simmer uncovered for another 20-30 minutes until the potatoes are cooked through and tender.
6. **Adjust seasoning:**

- Taste the broth and adjust the seasoning with salt if needed. You can also add more gochugaru for extra spiciness, if desired.
7. **Serve Gamjatang:**
    - Ladle the hot Gamjatang into individual bowls. Garnish with sesame seeds and sliced green onions.

Tips:

- **Meat options:** You can also use pork ribs or pork shoulder instead of pork bones for a meatier version of Gamjatang.
- **Kimchi:** Adding kimchi enhances the flavor of the soup and adds a hint of tanginess. Adjust the amount based on your preference.
- **Side dishes:** Serve Gamjatang with a bowl of steamed rice and traditional Korean side dishes (banchan) like kimchi, pickled radish, or seasoned vegetables.

Gamjatang is a robust and flavorful soup that's perfect for warming up on chilly days. Its combination of tender pork, spicy broth, and hearty vegetables makes it a satisfying meal that's enjoyed throughout Korea.

Ojingeochae Bokkeum (Stir-Fried Dried Squid)

Ingredients:

- 1 cup dried shredded squid (ojingeochae)
- 1 tablespoon vegetable oil
- 1 tablespoon soy sauce
- 1 tablespoon honey or sugar
- 1 tablespoon gochugaru (Korean red chili pepper flakes)
- 1 teaspoon sesame oil
- 1 teaspoon sesame seeds
- 2 cloves garlic, minced
- 1 green onion, chopped
- Optional: 1 teaspoon rice wine or mirin (for extra flavor)

Instructions:

1. **Prepare the dried squid:**
   - If the dried squid is very hard, soak it in warm water for about 10-15 minutes to soften. Drain and pat dry with paper towels.
2. **Slice the dried squid:**
   - Cut the dried squid into bite-sized pieces or strips, about 2-3 inches long.
3. **Stir-fry the squid:**
   - Heat vegetable oil in a large skillet or wok over medium heat.
   - Add minced garlic and stir-fry for about 30 seconds until fragrant.
4. **Add squid and seasonings:**
   - Add the dried squid pieces to the skillet. Stir-fry for 2-3 minutes until the squid starts to curl and become slightly crispy.
5. **Season the dish:**
   - In a small bowl, mix soy sauce, honey or sugar, gochugaru, sesame oil, and rice wine (if using).
   - Pour the sauce over the squid in the skillet. Stir-fry for another 2-3 minutes until the squid is well coated and heated through.
6. **Finish and garnish:**
   - Sprinkle sesame seeds and chopped green onion over the stir-fried squid.
   - Toss everything together for a final mix.
7. **Serve:**
   - Transfer ojingeochae bokkeum to a serving dish.
   - Serve hot or at room temperature as a side dish or snack.

Tips:

- **Adjust spice level:** You can adjust the amount of gochugaru (Korean red chili pepper flakes) depending on your spice preference. Add more for extra heat or reduce for a milder flavor.

- **Storage:** Store any leftovers in an airtight container in the refrigerator for up to 3-4 days. Reheat gently in a skillet or microwave before serving.

Ojingeochae bokkeum is a delightful Korean dish that combines the natural savory flavor of dried squid with a sweet-spicy sauce. It's quick and easy to make, perfect for adding variety to your Korean cuisine repertoire or as a tasty snack. Enjoy it with rice and other banchan dishes for a complete Korean meal experience!

Nakji Bokkeum (Stir-Fried Baby Octopus)

Ingredients:

- 1 lb baby octopus (nakji), cleaned and gutted
- 2 tablespoons vegetable oil
- 3 cloves garlic, minced
- 1 small onion, thinly sliced
- 1/2 cup chopped green onion
- 1/4 cup chopped carrot
- 1/4 cup chopped red bell pepper
- 1/4 cup chopped green bell pepper
- 1/4 cup gochujang (Korean red chili pepper paste)
- 2 tablespoons soy sauce
- 1 tablespoon honey or sugar
- 1 tablespoon sesame oil
- 1 teaspoon sesame seeds
- Optional: 1 tablespoon rice wine or mirin

Instructions:

1. **Prepare the baby octopus:**
   - Rinse the baby octopus under cold water and drain well. If they are large, you can slice them into smaller pieces.
2. **Stir-fry the octopus:**
   - Heat vegetable oil in a large skillet or wok over medium heat.
   - Add minced garlic and stir-fry for about 30 seconds until fragrant.
3. **Add vegetables:**
   - Add sliced onion, chopped green onion, chopped carrot, red bell pepper, and green bell pepper to the skillet. Stir-fry for 2-3 minutes until vegetables start to soften.
4. **Cook the octopus:**
   - Add the baby octopus to the skillet. Stir-fry for about 5-7 minutes until the octopus is cooked through and tender. Stir occasionally to ensure even cooking.
5. **Make the sauce:**
   - In a small bowl, mix together gochujang, soy sauce, honey or sugar, sesame oil, sesame seeds, and rice wine or mirin (if using). Adjust the sweetness and spiciness to taste.
6. **Combine and stir-fry:**
   - Pour the sauce over the octopus and vegetables in the skillet. Stir-fry everything together for another 2-3 minutes until well combined and heated through.
7. **Serve:**
   - Transfer nakji bokkeum to a serving dish.
   - Serve hot with steamed rice as a main dish or as a side dish (banchan).

Tips:

- **Cleaning octopus:** Ensure the baby octopus is thoroughly cleaned, removing any remaining innards and rinsing well under cold water.
- **Spice level:** Adjust the amount of gochujang and gochugaru (Korean red chili pepper flakes) according to your preference for spiciness.
- **Garnish:** Sprinkle additional sesame seeds and chopped green onion on top for garnish before serving.

Nakji bokkeum is a flavorful and satisfying dish that captures the essence of Korean cuisine with its bold flavors and tender octopus. Enjoy this dish as part of a Korean meal spread or as a standalone dish with rice!

Kimchi Mandu (Kimchi Dumplings)

Ingredients:

For the filling:

- 1 cup kimchi, finely chopped
- 1 cup firm tofu, drained and mashed
- 1/2 cup ground pork or beef (optional)
- 2 green onions, finely chopped
- 2 cloves garlic, minced
- 1 tablespoon soy sauce
- 1 tablespoon sesame oil
- 1 teaspoon sugar (optional, depending on the sweetness of your kimchi)
- 1/2 teaspoon ground black pepper
- 1/2 teaspoon salt, or to taste

For assembling:

- Round dumpling wrappers (store-bought or homemade)

For cooking:

- Vegetable oil (for pan-frying, if desired)
- Water (for steaming or boiling)

Instructions:

1. **Prepare the filling:**
    - Squeeze excess liquid from the chopped kimchi using your hands or a clean kitchen towel.
    - In a mixing bowl, combine chopped kimchi, mashed tofu, ground pork or beef (if using), green onions, minced garlic, soy sauce, sesame oil, sugar (if using), black pepper, and salt. Mix well until thoroughly combined.
2. **Assemble the dumplings:**
    - Take a dumpling wrapper and place a spoonful of the filling in the center (about 1 tablespoon).
    - Moisten the edges of the wrapper with water using your fingertip.
    - Fold the wrapper in half over the filling to create a half-moon shape, pressing the edges firmly to seal. You can also crimp the edges for a decorative look.
3. **Cooking options:**
    - **Steaming:** Place the dumplings in a steamer lined with parchment paper or cabbage leaves to prevent sticking. Steam for about 8-10 minutes until cooked through.
    - **Boiling:** Bring a pot of water to a boil. Carefully add the dumplings and cook until they float to the surface and the filling is cooked through, about 5-7 minutes.

- **Pan-frying (potstickers):** Heat a tablespoon of vegetable oil in a non-stick skillet over medium-high heat. Place the dumplings in the skillet in a single layer. Cook for 2-3 minutes until the bottoms are golden brown. Add 1/2 cup of water to the skillet, cover with a lid, and cook for another 5-7 minutes until the water is absorbed and the dumplings are crispy on the bottom.

4. **Serve:**
    - Arrange the cooked kimchi mandu on a serving platter.
    - Serve hot with dipping sauce such as soy sauce mixed with rice vinegar, or a spicy dipping sauce made with gochujang (Korean red chili paste) and sesame oil.

Tips:

- **Freezing:** If you want to freeze the dumplings for later, place them in a single layer on a baking sheet lined with parchment paper. Freeze until solid, then transfer to a freezer bag or container. They can be cooked directly from frozen, just increase the cooking time slightly.
- **Customization:** Feel free to adjust the filling ingredients according to your preference. You can make vegetarian kimchi mandu by omitting the meat and adding more tofu or vegetables.
- **Wrapping:** Ensure the dumplings are tightly sealed to prevent the filling from leaking during cooking.

Kimchi mandu are a delightful way to enjoy the spicy and tangy flavors of kimchi in a dumpling form. They're versatile and can be enjoyed as a snack, appetizer, or part of a larger Korean meal. Enjoy making and savoring these delicious dumplings at home!

Mul Naengmyeon (Cold Buckwheat Noodles in Broth)

Ingredients:

For the broth:

- 6 cups beef broth (or a combination of beef and anchovy broth)
- 1/4 cup soy sauce
- 2 tablespoons rice vinegar
- 2 tablespoons sugar
- 1 tablespoon sesame oil
- 1 tablespoon Korean mustard oil (gyeoja) or hot mustard paste (optional, for serving)
- 1 teaspoon minced garlic
- 1 teaspoon ginger, grated
- Salt and pepper, to taste

For serving:

- 4 bundles of dried naengmyeon noodles (buckwheat noodles)
- Hard-boiled eggs, halved
- Cucumber, julienned
- Korean pear or apple, thinly sliced
- Kimchi, optional
- Vinegar or spicy mustard sauce (yangnyeomjang), optional

Instructions:

1. **Prepare the broth:**
    - In a large pot, combine beef broth, soy sauce, rice vinegar, sugar, sesame oil, minced garlic, and grated ginger. Bring to a boil over medium-high heat.
    - Reduce the heat and simmer for about 15-20 minutes to allow the flavors to meld. Season with salt and pepper to taste. Remove from heat and let it cool completely.
    - Once cooled, refrigerate the broth until ready to serve. The broth should be well chilled before serving.
2. **Prepare the noodles:**
    - Cook the naengmyeon noodles according to the package instructions. Usually, this involves boiling them in water for about 3-5 minutes until they are cooked but still chewy (al dente).
    - Drain the noodles and rinse them under cold running water until they are completely cooled. Drain well again.
3. **Assemble mul naengmyeon:**
    - Divide the chilled noodles into individual serving bowls.
    - Pour the chilled broth over the noodles. The broth should generously cover the noodles.

        - Garnish with hard-boiled eggs (halved), julienned cucumber, and slices of Korean pear or apple.
        - Optionally, serve with kimchi on the side for extra flavor.
    4. **Serve:**
        - Serve mul naengmyeon immediately, offering Korean mustard oil (gyeoja) or hot mustard paste on the side for those who enjoy extra spice.
        - You can also offer vinegar or spicy mustard sauce (yangnyeomjang) as additional condiments for diners to adjust the flavor according to their taste preferences.

Tips:

- **Broth options:** Traditionally, beef broth is used for mul naengmyeon, but you can also use a combination of beef and anchovy broth for added depth of flavor.
- **Noodle variations:** Some variations include adding ice cubes to the broth to ensure it stays chilled, especially on hot days.
- **Make ahead:** You can prepare the broth and noodles ahead of time and assemble the dish just before serving for convenience.

Mul naengmyeon is a delightful dish that offers a perfect balance of savory, tangy, and refreshing flavors. It's a great choice for a light and cooling meal during warmer weather, and it's sure to be enjoyed by those who appreciate Korean cuisine.

Yangnyeom Tongdak (Korean Fried Chicken)

Ingredients:

For the chicken:

- 2 lbs chicken wings or drumsticks, washed and patted dry
- Salt and pepper, to taste
- 1 cup potato starch or cornstarch
- Vegetable oil, for frying

For the sauce:

- 3 tablespoons gochujang (Korean red chili pepper paste)
- 2 tablespoons gochugaru (Korean red chili pepper flakes)
- 2 tablespoons soy sauce
- 2 tablespoons rice vinegar
- 2 tablespoons honey or corn syrup
- 1 tablespoon sesame oil
- 4 cloves garlic, minced
- 1 tablespoon grated ginger
- 1 tablespoon brown sugar (optional, for extra sweetness)
- Toasted sesame seeds and chopped green onions, for garnish

Instructions:

1. **Prepare the chicken:**
    - Season the chicken pieces with salt and pepper.
    - Coat each piece evenly with potato starch or cornstarch, shaking off any excess.
2. **Fry the chicken:**
    - Heat vegetable oil in a deep fryer or large skillet to 350°F (175°C).
    - Carefully add the chicken pieces in batches and fry for about 10-12 minutes until golden brown and crispy. Make sure the chicken is cooked through (internal temperature should reach 165°F or 74°C). Drain on a wire rack or paper towels.
3. **Make the sauce:**
    - In a bowl, combine gochujang, gochugaru, soy sauce, rice vinegar, honey or corn syrup, sesame oil, minced garlic, grated ginger, and brown sugar (if using). Mix well until the sauce is smooth and well combined.
4. **Coat the chicken with sauce:**
    - In a large bowl, toss the fried chicken pieces with the prepared sauce until evenly coated. Alternatively, you can brush the sauce over the chicken pieces.
5. **Garnish and serve:**
    - Transfer the yangnyeom tongdak to a serving plate.
    - Sprinkle with toasted sesame seeds and chopped green onions for garnish.
6. **Serve immediately:**

- Enjoy the yangnyeom tongdak while it's hot and crispy. It pairs well with pickled radish (danmuji) and cold beer.

Tips:

- **Crispiness:** For extra crispy chicken, double fry the chicken pieces. After the first fry, let them cool slightly, then fry them again for another 3-5 minutes until they reach the desired crispiness.
- **Adjusting spice level:** Adjust the amount of gochugaru and gochujang according to your preference for spiciness. Add more for extra heat or reduce for a milder flavor.
- **Baking option:** If you prefer a healthier option, you can bake the chicken in the oven at 400°F (200°C) for 35-40 minutes, turning halfway through, until the chicken is cooked through and crispy. Toss with the sauce after baking.

Yangnyeom tongdak is a delightful Korean dish that's perfect for sharing with friends and family. The crispy chicken coated in the sweet and spicy sauce creates a flavor explosion that's sure to be a hit at any gathering or meal.

Ganjang Gejang (Soy Sauce Marinated Crabs)

Ingredients:

- 4-6 fresh blue crabs (female preferred for their roe), cleaned
- 1 cup soy sauce (preferably Korean soy sauce for soup or soy sauce for marinating)
- 1 cup water
- 1/2 cup vinegar (rice vinegar or apple cider vinegar)
- 1/2 cup sugar
- 4 cloves garlic, minced
- 1 small onion, thinly sliced
- 2 green onions, chopped
- 1 tablespoon sesame oil
- 1 tablespoon sesame seeds
- 1 tablespoon Korean red chili flakes (gochugaru), adjust to taste
- Optional: 1 tablespoon rice wine or soju

Instructions:

1. **Prepare the crabs:**
   - Clean the crabs thoroughly under cold running water to remove any dirt or impurities. Remove the top shell and gills. Cut each crab into halves or quarters, depending on their size. Keep the crab roe and other innards intact.
2. **Make the marinade:**
   - In a large mixing bowl, combine soy sauce, water, vinegar, sugar, minced garlic, sliced onion, chopped green onions, sesame oil, sesame seeds, Korean red chili flakes (gochugaru), and rice wine or soju (if using). Mix well until the sugar is dissolved and all ingredients are combined.
3. **Marinate the crabs:**
   - Place the cleaned crabs into a shallow dish or container with a lid.
   - Pour the marinade over the crabs, ensuring they are fully submerged. Cover the dish with plastic wrap or a lid.
4. **Refrigerate and marinate:**
   - Refrigerate the crabs for at least 24-48 hours (1-2 days), turning the crabs occasionally to ensure even marination. The longer they marinate, the more flavorful they will be.
5. **Serve:**
   - Remove the marinated crabs from the refrigerator and let them come to room temperature before serving.
   - Garnish with additional chopped green onions, sesame seeds, and Korean red chili flakes (gochugaru) if desired.
   - Serve ganjang gejang as a side dish (banchan) with steamed rice and other Korean side dishes.

Tips:

- **Freshness:** Use fresh and live crabs for the best flavor. Female crabs are preferred for their rich roe, which adds to the dish's flavor and texture.
- **Handling:** Be careful when handling raw crabs and their sharp shells. Use kitchen gloves or tongs if necessary.
- **Adjusting flavors:** Taste the marinade before adding the crabs and adjust the seasoning to your preference. You can add more sugar for sweetness or more gochugaru for spiciness.

Ganjang gejang is a delicacy in Korean cuisine, prized for its savory umami flavors and unique texture. It's enjoyed as a special treat during festive occasions or as a luxurious dish in Korean restaurants. Enjoy making and savoring this traditional Korean dish at home!

Gopchang Jeongol (Beef Intestine Hot Pot)

Ingredients:

- 1 lb beef intestines (gopchang), cleaned and prepared
- 1/2 lb beef brisket or sirloin, thinly sliced
- 1 onion, sliced
- 2-3 green onions, cut into 2-inch lengths
- 1 cup sliced mushrooms (shiitake or button mushrooms)
- 1 cup sliced Korean radish (mu)
- 1 cup sliced cabbage
- 4-5 cups beef broth or anchovy broth
- 2 tablespoons soy sauce
- 1 tablespoon gochugaru (Korean red chili pepper flakes)
- 1 tablespoon minced garlic
- 1 tablespoon sesame oil
- 1 tablespoon rice wine (mirin) or soju (optional)
- Salt and pepper, to taste
- Kimchi, for serving (optional)
- Cooked rice, for serving

Instructions:

1. **Prepare the beef intestines:**
    - Clean the beef intestines thoroughly under cold running water. Soak them in cold water with a bit of vinegar for about 30 minutes to remove any odor. Rinse well and drain.
2. **Prepare the broth:**
    - In a large pot or Korean earthenware pot (ttukbaegi), bring the beef broth or anchovy broth to a boil over medium-high heat.
3. **Season the broth:**
    - Add soy sauce, gochugaru, minced garlic, sesame oil, and rice wine (if using) to the boiling broth. Stir well to combine.
    - Season with salt and pepper to taste.
4. **Add ingredients to the pot:**
    - Add the beef intestines, sliced beef brisket or sirloin, sliced onion, green onions, mushrooms, Korean radish, and cabbage to the pot. Arrange them evenly.
5. **Simmer and cook:**
    - Reduce the heat to medium-low and simmer the hot pot for about 20-25 minutes, or until the beef and vegetables are cooked through and tender.
    - Stir occasionally to ensure even cooking and flavors.
6. **Serve:**
    - Serve gopchang jeongol hot directly from the pot.
    - Enjoy with steamed rice and kimchi on the side, if desired.

Tips:

- **Preparation of beef intestines:** If you're not familiar with cleaning and preparing beef intestines, you can ask your butcher to clean them for you. Make sure to rinse them thoroughly before cooking.
- **Variations:** You can customize the vegetables and meat according to your preference. Some variations include adding tofu, enoki mushrooms, or other seasonal vegetables.
- **Spice level:** Adjust the amount of gochugaru according to your spice preference. You can add more for a spicier hot pot or reduce it for a milder flavor.

Gopchang jeongol is a comforting and flavorful dish that's perfect for sharing with family and friends. It's often enjoyed during colder months in Korea but can be enjoyed any time of year for its hearty and satisfying qualities. Enjoy the rich flavors of this traditional Korean hot pot!

Guljeon (Oyster Pancakes)

Ingredients:

- 1 cup all-purpose flour
- 1 cup water
- 1 egg
- 1/2 teaspoon salt
- 1/4 teaspoon black pepper
- 1/2 cup chopped green onions
- 1/2 cup thinly sliced carrots
- 1/2 cup thinly sliced bell pepper (optional)
- 1/2 cup thinly sliced onion
- 1 cup fresh oysters, shucked and drained
- Vegetable oil, for frying
- Soy sauce or vinegar dipping sauce, for serving

Instructions:

1. **Prepare the batter:**
    - In a large mixing bowl, combine flour, water, egg, salt, and black pepper. Whisk until smooth and well combined.
2. **Add vegetables and oysters:**
    - Stir in chopped green onions, sliced carrots, bell pepper (if using), and sliced onion into the batter.
    - Gently fold in the fresh oysters until evenly distributed in the batter.
3. **Cook the pancakes:**
    - Heat a large non-stick skillet or frying pan over medium heat. Add enough vegetable oil to coat the bottom of the pan.
    - Spoon a ladleful of batter onto the hot skillet, spreading it out to form a round pancake (about 4-6 inches in diameter).
    - Cook for 3-4 minutes on each side, or until golden brown and crispy. Use a spatula to carefully flip the pancake.
4. **Repeat:**
    - Repeat with the remaining batter, adding more oil to the pan as needed. Cook pancakes in batches, depending on the size of your skillet.
5. **Serve:**
    - Serve guljeon hot, garnished with extra chopped green onions if desired.
    - Serve with soy sauce or vinegar dipping sauce on the side for extra flavor.

Tips:

- **Fresh oysters:** Use fresh oysters for the best flavor and texture. Make sure to drain them well before adding to the batter.

- **Vegetable variations:** You can customize the vegetables according to your preference. Some recipes include mushrooms or zucchini as well.
- **Crispy texture:** For extra crispiness, make sure the skillet is hot enough before adding the batter, and use enough oil to fry the pancakes evenly.

Guljeon is a delicious Korean dish that's perfect as an appetizer or side dish. The combination of crispy pancake batter and tender oysters with vegetables makes it a delightful treat enjoyed by many. Serve it as part of a Korean meal or as a special dish for gatherings and celebrations.

Dubu Kimchi (Stir-Fried Tofu with Kimchi)

Ingredients:

- 1 block (14-16 oz) soft tofu (silken or regular), cut into cubes
- 1 cup kimchi, chopped
- 1 tablespoon gochujang (Korean red chili paste)
- 1 tablespoon soy sauce
- 1 tablespoon sesame oil
- 1 tablespoon vegetable oil
- 2 green onions, chopped (white and green parts separated)
- 2 cloves garlic, minced
- 1 teaspoon sesame seeds, for garnish
- Optional: 1 teaspoon sugar (to balance the flavors if kimchi is too sour)
- Optional: 1 teaspoon rice vinegar or mirin (for added sweetness and tanginess)

Instructions:

1. **Prepare the tofu:**
    - Cut the tofu into bite-sized cubes and set aside.
2. **Stir-fry the tofu:**
    - Heat vegetable oil in a large skillet or pan over medium heat.
    - Add the tofu cubes to the skillet and cook for about 4-5 minutes, gently turning occasionally, until lightly browned on all sides. Remove tofu from the skillet and set aside.
3. **Prepare the sauce:**
    - In the same skillet, add sesame oil and heat over medium heat.
    - Add minced garlic and the white parts of the green onions. Sauté for about 1-2 minutes until fragrant.
4. **Add kimchi and seasoning:**
    - Add chopped kimchi to the skillet and stir-fry for another 3-4 minutes until the kimchi is heated through and starts to caramelize slightly.
    - Stir in gochujang, soy sauce, and optional sugar and rice vinegar or mirin (if using). Mix well to combine with the kimchi.
5. **Combine tofu and kimchi:**
    - Gently add the cooked tofu cubes back into the skillet with the kimchi mixture. Toss gently to coat the tofu evenly with the sauce. Cook for another 2-3 minutes until heated through.
6. **Serve:**
    - Transfer dubu kimchi to a serving dish.
    - Garnish with chopped green onions (green parts) and sesame seeds.

Tips:

- **Tofu:** Use soft or silken tofu for a smoother texture. Firm tofu can also be used if you prefer a chewier texture.
- **Spice level:** Adjust the amount of gochujang according to your spice preference. You can add more for extra heat or reduce for a milder flavor.
- **Serve with:** Dubu kimchi is delicious served hot as a main dish with steamed rice. It can also be served as a side dish (banchan) alongside other Korean dishes.

Dubu kimchi is a comforting and flavorful dish that highlights the bold flavors of kimchi and the delicate texture of tofu. Enjoy this Korean classic at home for a satisfying and easy-to-make meal!

Dak Bulgogi (Spicy Chicken BBQ)

Ingredients:

- 1 lb (450g) chicken breast or thigh, thinly sliced
- 3 tablespoons gochujang (Korean chili paste)
- 2 tablespoons soy sauce
- 1 tablespoon honey or sugar
- 1 tablespoon sesame oil
- 3 cloves garlic, minced
- 1 teaspoon ginger, minced
- 1 tablespoon vegetable oil, for cooking
- 1 onion, thinly sliced
- 2-3 green onions, chopped (for garnish)
- Sesame seeds (for garnish, optional)

Instructions:

1. **Prepare the Marinade:**
    - In a bowl, mix together gochujang, soy sauce, honey (or sugar), sesame oil, minced garlic, and minced ginger. Adjust the amount of gochujang based on your spice preference.
2. **Marinate the Chicken:**
    - Add the thinly sliced chicken to the marinade and mix well, ensuring each piece is coated evenly. Cover and refrigerate for at least 30 minutes to allow the flavors to meld.
3. **Cooking:**
    - Heat vegetable oil in a large skillet or wok over medium-high heat.
    - Add sliced onions and cook until they start to soften, about 2-3 minutes.
4. **Add Chicken:**
    - Add the marinated chicken to the skillet. Cook, stirring frequently, until the chicken is cooked through and nicely caramelized, about 6-8 minutes.
5. **Finish and Serve:**
    - Garnish with chopped green onions and sesame seeds if desired.
    - Serve hot with steamed rice and your favorite Korean side dishes like kimchi or pickled vegetables.

Enjoy your Dak Bulgogi! It's spicy, flavorful, and perfect for a satisfying meal.

Saengseon Jeon (Pan-Fried Fish Cakes)

Ingredients:

- 250g fish fillets (such as cod or any white fish), deboned and skinned
- 2 tablespoons potato starch (or cornstarch)
- 1 egg
- 2 tablespoons finely chopped spring onions (green onions)
- 1 tablespoon finely chopped carrot (optional)
- 1 tablespoon finely chopped red bell pepper (optional)
- Salt and pepper, to taste
- Vegetable oil, for frying

Dipping Sauce:

- 2 tablespoons soy sauce
- 1 tablespoon water
- 1 teaspoon rice vinegar
- 1 teaspoon sesame oil
- 1 teaspoon sugar
- 1 teaspoon sesame seeds (optional)
- Pinch of red pepper flakes (optional)

Instructions:

1. **Prepare the Fish:**
   - Cut the fish fillets into chunks and place them in a food processor.
   - Pulse until the fish turns into a smooth paste. Alternatively, you can finely chop the fish with a knife until it becomes a paste-like consistency.
2. **Mix the Batter:**
   - In a mixing bowl, combine the fish paste with potato starch (or cornstarch), egg, chopped spring onions, chopped carrot, chopped red bell pepper (if using), salt, and pepper. Mix well until everything is evenly combined.
3. **Form the Fish Cakes:**
   - Heat vegetable oil in a frying pan over medium-high heat.
   - Take a spoonful of the fish mixture and gently flatten it to form a small patty (about 2-3 inches in diameter). Repeat with the remaining mixture, placing the patties in the hot oil.
4. **Fry the Fish Cakes:**
   - Fry the fish cakes for about 3-4 minutes on each side, or until they are golden brown and cooked through. Be careful not to overcrowd the pan; you may need to fry them in batches.
5. **Make the Dipping Sauce:**

- While the fish cakes are frying, prepare the dipping sauce by mixing soy sauce, water, rice vinegar, sesame oil, sugar, sesame seeds (if using), and red pepper flakes (if using) in a small bowl. Stir until the sugar is dissolved.
6. **Serve:**
    - Once the fish cakes are cooked, transfer them to a plate lined with paper towels to drain excess oil.
    - Serve hot with the dipping sauce on the side.

Enjoy your Saengseon Jeon as a delicious Korean appetizer or side dish! The crispy exterior and tender interior, combined with the savory dipping sauce, make it a delightful treat.

Yukhoe (Korean Beef Tartare)

Ingredients:

- 200g beef tenderloin or sirloin, very finely sliced or minced
- 1 egg yolk
- 1 tablespoon soy sauce
- 1 teaspoon sesame oil
- 1 teaspoon sugar
- 1/2 teaspoon honey
- 1/2 teaspoon minced garlic
- 1/2 teaspoon minced ginger
- 1/2 teaspoon sesame seeds
- 1/2 teaspoon ground black pepper
- 1/2 pear, peeled and finely grated (optional)
- 1/2 cucumber, julienned (for garnish)
- 1 tablespoon pine nuts, toasted (for garnish, optional)
- Thinly sliced green onion (for garnish)
- Korean pear or apple slices (for serving, optional)

Instructions:

1. **Prepare the Beef:**
   - Start with a very cold piece of beef. It's crucial to ensure that the beef is fresh and high-quality.
   - Trim off any excess fat and sinew. Slice the beef very thinly against the grain or finely mince it with a sharp knife.
2. **Prepare the Sauce:**
   - In a bowl, combine soy sauce, sesame oil, sugar, honey, minced garlic, minced ginger, sesame seeds, and ground black pepper. Mix well until the sugar dissolves.
3. **Marinate the Beef:**
   - Place the sliced or minced beef in a bowl. Add the egg yolk and gently mix it with the beef.
   - Pour the sauce over the beef and mix well to ensure all pieces are coated evenly.
   - If using grated pear, add it to the beef mixture and mix gently. The pear adds a hint of sweetness and helps tenderize the meat.
4. **Serve:**
   - Arrange the marinated beef on a plate, shaping it neatly if desired.
   - Garnish with julienned cucumber, toasted pine nuts, thinly sliced green onion, and Korean pear or apple slices.
   - Serve immediately as an appetizer. Yukhoe is traditionally enjoyed with a bowl of rice or as part of a Korean meal spread.

Tips:

- **Freshness:** Use fresh, high-quality beef for the best flavor and texture.
- **Safety:** If you have concerns about consuming raw meat, choose beef labeled specifically for tartare or carpaccio, or consult your butcher.
- **Presentation:** Yukhoe is often served beautifully arranged on a plate, making it visually appealing as well as delicious.

Enjoy your Yukhoe as a sophisticated and flavorful Korean dish that showcases the delicate flavors of raw beef combined with savory and aromatic seasonings.

Gaji Namul (Seasoned Eggplant)

Ingredients:

- 2 medium-sized Asian eggplants (or 1 large Italian eggplant)
- 1 tablespoon soy sauce
- 1 tablespoon sesame oil
- 1 tablespoon sesame seeds
- 1 clove garlic, minced
- 1 green onion, finely chopped
- 1 teaspoon sugar (optional)
- Salt, to taste
- Vegetable oil, for cooking

Instructions:

1. **Prepare the Eggplant:**
   - Rinse the eggplants under cold water. Trim off the stem ends.
   - Cut the eggplants into thin strips or slices. You can cut them into rounds or julienne them, depending on your preference.
2. **Blanch the Eggplant:**
   - Bring a pot of water to a boil. Add a pinch of salt.
   - Add the eggplant slices to the boiling water and blanch for about 1-2 minutes, or until they are tender but still slightly firm.
   - Drain the eggplants and rinse them under cold water to stop the cooking process. Drain well and gently squeeze out any excess water.
3. **Seasoning:**
   - In a mixing bowl, combine soy sauce, sesame oil, sesame seeds, minced garlic, chopped green onion, and sugar (if using). Mix well to combine all the ingredients.
4. **Cooking:**
   - Heat a small amount of vegetable oil in a skillet or frying pan over medium heat.
   - Add the blanched eggplant slices to the skillet and stir-fry for about 2-3 minutes, or until they are heated through and lightly coated with oil.
5. **Combine with Seasoning:**
   - Remove the skillet from heat. Pour the prepared seasoning mixture over the cooked eggplant slices.
   - Gently toss the eggplant slices with the seasoning until they are evenly coated.
6. **Serve:**
   - Transfer the seasoned eggplant to a serving dish.
   - Garnish with additional sesame seeds and chopped green onions if desired.
   - Serve Gaji Namul warm or at room temperature as a delicious side dish alongside steamed rice and other Korean dishes.

Tips:

- **Eggplant Selection:** Asian eggplants are ideal for this dish because they are tender and cook quickly. However, you can also use Italian eggplants if Asian eggplants are not available.
- **Seasoning Adjustments:** Taste the dish before serving and adjust the seasoning to your preference. You can add a little more soy sauce, sesame oil, or sugar according to your taste.
- **Storage:** Leftovers can be stored in an airtight container in the refrigerator for up to 2-3 days. Reheat gently before serving.

Enjoy making and savoring Gaji Namul as a flavorful addition to your Korean meal!

Maeuntang (Spicy Fish Stew)

Ingredients:

- 1 lb (450g) white fish fillets (such as cod, halibut, or snapper), cut into chunks
- 6 cups water or fish stock
- 1 onion, thinly sliced
- 1 green onion, cut into 2-inch pieces
- 1/2 block (about 4 oz) firm tofu, cut into cubes
- 1/2 cup sliced Korean radish (or daikon radish)
- 1/2 cup sliced carrot
- 1/2 cup sliced zucchini
- 4-5 dried red chili peppers, cut into halves and deseeded
- 3 tablespoons gochugaru (Korean red chili pepper flakes)
- 2 tablespoons gochujang (Korean chili paste)
- 2 tablespoons soy sauce
- 1 tablespoon minced garlic
- 1 tablespoon fish sauce
- 1 tablespoon sesame oil
- 1 tablespoon cooking oil
- Salt and pepper, to taste
- Fresh cilantro or chopped green onion for garnish (optional)

Instructions:

1. **Prepare the Broth:**
   - In a large pot, heat cooking oil over medium heat. Add sliced onion and green onion pieces. Saute for 2-3 minutes until onions are translucent.
2. **Make the Seasoning Paste:**
   - In a small bowl, mix together gochugaru (Korean red chili pepper flakes), gochujang (Korean chili paste), soy sauce, minced garlic, fish sauce, and sesame oil to make a paste.
3. **Cook the Stew:**
   - Add water or fish stock to the pot with the sauteed onions. Bring to a boil.
   - Add sliced radish, carrot, zucchini, and dried red chili peppers to the pot. Simmer for about 5 minutes until the vegetables start to soften.
4. **Add Fish and Tofu:**
   - Gently add the fish chunks and tofu cubes to the pot. Simmer for another 5-7 minutes, or until the fish is cooked through and flakes easily with a fork.
5. **Season and Adjust:**
   - Stir in the seasoning paste (from step 2) into the stew. Taste and adjust the seasoning with salt and pepper if needed. You can add more gochugaru or gochujang for extra spiciness, if desired.
6. **Serve:**

- Ladle the Maeuntang into individual bowls. Garnish with fresh cilantro or chopped green onion, if desired.
- Serve hot with steamed rice and other side dishes. Maeuntang is often enjoyed as a main dish in a Korean meal.

Tips:

- **Seafood Variation:** You can add other types of seafood such as shrimp, mussels, or squid to the stew for a richer flavor.
- **Adjust Spiciness:** The spiciness of Maeuntang can be adjusted according to your preference. Add more or less gochugaru and gochujang to suit your taste.
- **Leftovers:** Maeuntang can be stored in the refrigerator for a day or two. Reheat gently on the stove before serving.

Enjoy preparing and savoring Maeuntang, a hearty and comforting Korean spicy fish stew that's perfect for any occasion!

www.ingramcontent.com/pod-product-compliance
Lightning Source LLC
LaVergne TN
LVHW061942070526
838199LV00060B/3934